SOUL AND SENSUALITY

Returning the Erotic to
Everyday Life

Roger Housden

RIDER
London

First published in 1993 by Rider,
An imprint of Random House Ltd,
20 Vauxhall Bridge Road, London SW1V 2SA

Random Century Group Australia (Pty) Ltd,
20 Alfred Street, Milsons Point,
Sydney, NSW 2061, Australia

Random Century New Zealand Ltd,
18 Poland Road, Glenfield
Auckland 10, New Zealand

Random Century Group South Africa (Pty) Ltd,
PO Box 337, Bergvlei 2012, South Africa

Printed and bound in England by Mackays of Chatham PLC,
Chatham, Kent.

A catalogue record for this book is available
from the British Library.

ISBN 0 7126 5392 90 (paper)

AUTHOR'S NOTE

My gratitude extends first and foremost to Chloe Goodchild for consenting so readily to allow aspects of our life together to emerge as material for this book; for her encouragement, and for her valuable input as a critical reader. Peter Hawkins was also a reader whose suggestions and ideas I have appreciated and incorporated. Tessa Strickland has been the model of a project editor, willing to stretch far beyond my original brief, encouraging the imaginative process throughout, and giving thought and consideration to every aspect of the project. Jane Birdsell's final editing has significantly improved the text; and I could not have wished for a more beautiful cover than the one designed by Elaine Cox. Last but not least, I acknowledge my debt to the parts of the world which have inspired so much of this book; and to Nature in general which has never failed to offer me food for thought and heart.

While everything in this book is based on personal experience and aspires to poetic truth, I have occasionally made use of artistic licence with the factual details.

CONTENTS

CONTENTS

THE EROTIC LIFE

I wrote a story of the Resurrection, where Jesus gets up and feels very sick about everything and can't stand the old crowd any more – so cuts out – and as he heals up, he begins to find what an astonishing place the phenomenal world is, far more marvellous than any salvation or heaven – and thanks his stars that he needn't have a mission any more.

D.H. Lawrence in a letter to Earl Brewster, 1926[1]

Let me tell you the other story of Eve. Eve did a brave and beautiful thing. She reached her arm past the injunctions of the Father God, she picked the apple from the tree, and bit into its ripe and ready flesh. She knew that it was good, and she passed the apple on to Adam, that he might taste the goodness of it also. In that moment, Adam and Eve awoke from the primordial dream, and their eyes were opened. They saw the beauty of their form in the splendour of their own light.

Now Eve was wise from the very beginning. She had a great friend in the garden, the most subtle of all the creatures. This was the snake, who kept close to the ground and knew the ways of the inner worlds that ran deep in the earth and ensured the plants and the trees grew according to their season. The snake was brimming with life from his many wanderings, and his wisdom was in the words that he whispered to Eve when he advised her to eat the apple. Eve was wise because she was able to listen deeply. Eve listened, and beneath the clamour of the Father voice which told her to do its bidding without questioning she could hear the softer whisperings of a truer life. Eve chose this way of life, according to her own conscience, and she took the fruit.

In that one moment, Eve blessed all generations to come with the gift of being able to take part in the creation of their own world. When the snake slipped his word into Eve's ear he fertilized her sleeping soul. She could see then with an inner seeing, and it was in the light of that intelligence thatshe chose her way.

Now Eve is the living soul of a human being, and as such, she has had many names. The ancient peoples of Greece called her Psyche. Psyche, too, saw with an inner eye, as we know from her adventure with Eros. When the god, Eros,[2] fell in love with Psyche, he led her into the Valley of Paradise. Every night he visited her, and asked for just one promise in return, to ensure they would continue to live in eternal happiness. Eros said she was not to look at him or inquire into any of his ways. She could have anything she wished, except the knowledge of who he was. Psyche agreed not to ask questions. She liked the Paradise he had taken her to, where all her needs were met. But then Psyche was moved by her inner doubts to shine a lamp on Eros, and she saw that he was a beautiful god. She immediately fell in love with him; but Eros, revealed for who he was, fled from Paradise. Psyche followed him, and fell to earth.

She was no longer the same, though, as she had been before: the touch of love had awoken her soul. She knew Eros now, and was awakened to the erotic life. Psyche, the human, could see with a godlike eye life's wonders and possibilities. She could feel a delight and a love that at times were almost too much for her mortal frame to bear. Life flowed in its fullness through her heart and her senses. No longer alone in a world apart (in Paradise), her love brought her close to life. She could feel and value the press of the earth beneath her feet, the beauty of two people making love, the life in a wayside stone or shrub. Psyche's knowing, like Eve's, proceeded not from thought, but from a larger intelligence which knows where it is going, in the same way a river does. The erotic is a show of soul, whose light can see and value the heart of life.

Eve 'knew' to take the apple. She had the greatness of heart to reach out her hand in the face of all reason. Eve had courage because she knew that in eating the fruit of a conscious life she would be living the pain as well as the joy. Inevitably, a terrible thing came to pass. For thousands of years the name of Eve was blackened and reviled. She dared to disturb the peace, to go against the prevailing wisdom of the time. She had the temerity not to stay in her place, and there was a certain price to pay. The Christian Church[3] took on the stern voice of Jehovah as soon as one of its saints, Augustine, proclaimed that Eve was not, after all, a bestower of life but a perpetrator of the original sin, passed down to us all ever since. From Augustine on, the wisdom of Eve was reviled. The beauty and life of the manifest world came to be seen as temptations drawing the spirit away from its true home in some heaven that would only be fully appreciated in the afterlife. Body and spirit were separated, and the soul was chased out of this world. The world of living beings, including the human body itself, became a world of things, of objects devoid of their own meaning and intelligence. The animals and the trees fell silent. Life was carved into two: right and wrong, good and bad, spiritual and carnal. This was the true act of original sin. Endless sufferings have trailed in its wake, most of them in the name of righteousness.

So the erotic life was trampled underfoot, or held hostage behind tight lips and prim and proper façades. Nowadays, it is concealed in even cleverer ways. Sex and pornography are a booming business, which only goes to show, some people say, what a liberated and sensual culture we are. But pornography divorces body from soul and turns the body into a thing, which can be used like any other thing for profit in the market-place. Pornography is a caricature of the erotic: it can only exist by denying relationship. It demands anonymity, as Eros did before Psyche shone her light on him. Without relationship, there is no connectedness, no feeling, and no valuing of the other person. There is no soul. There is only sensation, for its own sake. Sensation is only skin-deep; its effects are im-mediate and short-term, and like a ride on the big dipper, its risks are mostly hypothetical, rather than real. Sensation, un-like the erotic, lets us off lightly. There is nothing to give, ex-cept the cost of the ride. To skim the surface of life, however, leaves us on our own, and ultimately lonely. Far from being an erotic culture, we are probably one of the most disembodied and anti-sensual cultures of all time.

We lose touch with our senses when we settle for sensa-tion alone, or when we content ourselves with the fantasy of something, rather than with the thing itself. We can be so absorbed in our image of the pleasure of chocolate, for example, that we lose all contact with our body and do not even know whether it actually considers chocolate pleasurable or not. Consumerism is not a result of the body's appetites; it is sustained by the artificial stimulation and creation of desires. If we allowed ourselves to savour more, we would undoubtedly buy less.

We would buy less because a genuine pleasure is *full-filling*; it is the perfectly natural and healthy satisfaction in the exchange between the senses and the surrounding world. When Psyche left the Vale of Paradise and returned to earth, she gave birth to the child of Eros, Pleasure. Pleasure is an awareness of the passage of Eros. It is an erotic response to life, one that is physically moving. The body shudders, quivers, and trembles with pleasure. Like 'erotic', it is a word that has lost its original savour. The litmus test for a sin in the Catholic Church is still the question, 'Did you take pleasure in it?'

Pathos and pain are as much part of an erotic life as joy and pleasure. Eve took on the responsibility for her consciousness and suffered the pain of childbirth and eventual death. There is great pathos – a richness of feeling that could be called passion as well as suffering – in every transition from innocence to knowledge. Many of us have suffered the passion of moving from the bliss of romantic love to the more sober work of forging an enduring relationship. Suffering of this kind has vitality; it can help the light of a person to shine more strongly.

Both pathos and pleasure are bodily knowings. They are sensuous and sensual experiences, living proof that we are alive, and in touch with the rest of life. This is the case if

Psyche's lamp is shining. If the heart is asleep, pathos becomes sheer pain, and pain and pleasure remain at the level of sensation. When the heroines in the film *Thelma and Louise* decide to break out of the stifling conformity of their small Southern town in the United States, they start out in true adventurous style, leaving no note and not knowing where they will end up for the night. They soon find trouble, and one trouble leads to another. The excitement of trouble can be addictive, and during the course of their journey Thelma and Louise metamorphose from dumb blondes into wild and reckless women on the run, with several state police departments on their tail. The film ends with the ultimate wildness of driving their car over a cliff.

Thelma and Louise took their courage in their hands and, like Eve, they defied the dominating patriarchy of their time. They defied husband and lover, and went in the face of law and order. However, the joy of their liberation soon turned to violence and they eventually turned their violence on themselves, taking their own lives. Violence can be the flip side of joy. The unfettered aliveness of the erotic current will turn to violence, madness, or death, if it is without any guiding light. Irrationality, it turns out, is no valid replacement for rationalism. The film is profoundly moving in a tragic way. It seems to show no alternative to the stereotypes of male abuse of power versus the female furies. Thelma and Louise were desperate to feel life coursing through their hearts and minds. Like drug addicts and alcoholics – like all of us in our own less obvious ways – they were longing for the ecstasy of a full-blooded life.

Sensation on its own – however orgasmic – ultimately fails to deliver the goods. One reason we seem to be such a pleasure-hungry society is that we are habitually looking for it in the wrong places. The shiny surface of life will always bounce us from pain to pleasure, rationality to irrationality, good to bad, and back again. The deeper connections and currents between things take place below the skin, and they are illuminated by the softer light that Eve brought into the world – not the power of a spotlight, or the cutting edge of a laser beam, but rather the more feminine light of a candle, or a lamp, such as Psyche shone on to Eros. This light from the erotic heart is more diffuse, altogether softer, letting things remain in their surroundings rather than picking them out. Instead of being judgemental, it is receptive and discerning. Instead of destroying, it warms the world.

This is the light that connects us to life's intelligent ways. Rather than being something we can turn on or off at will, it is a knowing that we can participate in. We tend to live collectively in the myth of self-determination, with the idea of ourselves being in control, and at the helm of our lives. But Eve did not rationally choose her way as a conscious ego; she let life choose her, seeing that it was good. She willingly played her part in the unfolding of a larger story which had its own intentionality and logic. We are part of that same story now, as it is unfolding in our time. At a more local level, we are part of a network of lives – our family, friends, enemies, and colleagues – that make up our own personal story. The erotic soul is not something we have; we are immersed in it.

> We labour under the misapprehension that we have to think up what we have to do. The truth is that this is not our responsibility, because the pattern of things is far greater than we can imagine . . . . The direct perception of our pattern belongs to conscience – the unconditioned side of our nature. The pattern is creative and created.'
>
> **J.G. Bennett, *The Way to be Free*[3]**

What Bennett calls conscience, I call soul, and soul is the source of the erotic. It is what sees through the names of things, their literal and concrete reality, to the deeper pattern of which they are a part. When suffering and joy stream from the soul they are a way, not of losing ourselves, but of finding ourselves. It is soul, imagination, that brings the opposites into relationship. Body and mind are brought together by the inner eye. In its presence, the body is as sacred as any holy place, and through the conduit of the senses, the light of the person flows into the light of the world.

This book is a journey through each of the senses. It explores how we may taste, smell, touch, hear and see more deeply of the world, and how the senses can bring the inner and the outer together. It seeks to foster a love of the beauty of everyday life and of living it, the pathos and pleasure of it, the sensuality and sacredness of it. It is a celebration of the erotic in life.

$\mathcal{T}$ASTING

People ask me: Why do you write about food, and eating and drinking? Why don't you write about the struggle for power and security, and about love, the way others do? They ask it accusingly, as if I were somehow gross, unfaithful to the honor of my craft.

The easiest answer is to say that, like most other humans, I am hungry. But there is more than that. It seems to me that our three basic needs, for food and security and love, are so mixed and mingled and entwined that we cannot straightly think of one without the others. So it happens that when I write of hunger, I am really writing about love and the hunger for it, and warmth and the love of it and the hunger for it . . . and then the warmth and richness and fine reality of hunger satisfied . . . and it is all one.

M.F.K. Fisher, *The Art of Eating*[1]

TASTE MEMORIES

the milk of a dandelion stalk

iron in the desert air

salt in the wind

apple crumble

lemon in tea

soft white bread made with overnight dough

a bitter pill

a stem of grass

the end of my pencil

geranium leaves

fresh ginger

an oyster

warm water from a drinking fountain

rancid butter

sulphur in a hot spring

fresh thyme

mouthfuls of dust in Ladakh

codliver oil

a wild strawberry

a wet sponge in the bath

blood pouring from the end of my finger

a soft school rubber

mango

bay leaves

soggy potatoes for school lunch

a bite into a bitter sloe

maple syrup

When Enough Is Enough

Aerobics, callisthenics, work-outs, none of them have made much of a lasting impression on the shape of the Western body. The developed nations are growing fatter by the year, while much of the rest of the world is growing thinner, even to the point of starvation. Why do we do it to ourselves? Why have I spoiled a thousand dinners by taking just those two or three mouthfuls too many? Mostly, because I have not paid attention. I have not been in touch with my body. I have been consumed by the enjoyment of what I was eating, so that in truth it was eating me. The thought has passed through my mind over and over again that another mouthful wouldn't hurt. I have justified that thought as self-tolerance; I have put it down to a healthy enthusiasm for the delights of the table. Its proper name, I know, is greed.

We have all been greedy at one time or another, and not only in some sudden enthusiasm for a delicious food. Greed stretches deeper than gourmandize. Many of us feel at times like a bottomless pit, the filling of which our contentment appears to depend upon. More food, more clothes, more things for the house – 'keep shopping' is our culture's motto. Anything to fill The Gap. The feeling of completeness, fulfilment, is what we want, and if we can't get the real thing, the next best is a snack, or even better, a full stomach, which blots out (more or less, and only for three hours) the anxiety that surrounds the feeling of lack, the empty void. Food is intimately connected to the feeling of The Gap because prolonged lack of food results in the ultimate gap of death. Psyche and soma are so subtly implicated in each other that a psychic sense of emptiness or unfulfilment naturally constellates into the thought that an empty stomach is needing to be filled. A preoccupation with the accumulation of material goods is an extension of the same need. The roots of greed are deep indeed.

Overeating anaesthetizes us to the life that wants to move through our body. It is anti-erotic; it subdues what we really want, the feeling of life in our veins. It is a short step from there to a feeling of guilt, and our consequent preoccupation with diets. Every month a new one hits the women's magazines. Yet gradually we are coming to see that diets are not the answer. They are simply the corollary of overeating. The one invites the other. Both are fuelled by obsessional and compulsive patterns of behaviour. Both can escalate to the chronic disorders of bulimia and anorexia, the anguished cries of a beleaguered soul so movingly and powerfully described by Marion Woodman in her books.[2]

There are now popular movements among women in Britain and the United States to reject diets and to celebrate the way they are, whatever shape they may be. There is a backlash against the glossy image of the lean young frame that few people – for genetic reasons, quite apart from what they may eat – are ever able to acquire. The skinny look is increasingly been seen as a tyrannical product of fashion, and not as a prerequisite for beauty.

The fact remains, however, that both men and women in the developed world are often too fat for their own good, quite apart from prevailing images in fashion. Heart failure is our number one killer. The vast majority of us lead sedentary lives and eat a diet heavily weighed down by refined sugar and starches. This bland, gooey fare bears a resemblance to baby food, and it is hardly surprising that so many of us still have puppy fat in our thirties and forties. I am tempted to think that all this sucking and chewing of mints and sweets, chocolate bars and snacks, helps to keep many of us in a vicious circle of emotional dependency and narcissistic behaviour. If it is true that we are what we eat, then most of us are pegged at a level of emotional maturity no greater than that of young children.

Our eating habits, then – not just what we eat, but how much we eat, the way we eat (fast), and where we eat (for millions, in front of the television) all conspire to turn one of the most sensuous and pleasurable experiences of human existence into a neurotic, disembodied fuelling of a machine whose appetites have run away with its owner. The body is *not* a machine! The mechanical analogy is an anachronistic residue of Newtonian thinking which continues to perpetrate untold damage on our physical existence and, specifically, to rationalize behaviour that treats the human organism with a lack of regard that would be an insult to a combustion engine.

We do not exist separately from our bodies. Neither do we exist in our brain cells alone, as if the rest of our physical being were a mere appendage to carry us about and gratify our desires. Our body is a dimension of who we are, an integral part of our humanity. To contract our sense of identity into one end of it, the head, is to follow the compartmentalized view of reality that is the legacy of the eighteenth century Enlightenment. That legacy has given us the billiard-ball model of existence, in which people and objects are separate packages which bounce off each other without any relational existence. In this view, the body is simply another object. 'We' are the light of reason, and we live in the splendid isolation of the cortex. The more we retreat like this into a corner of ourselves, the more we live and experience life like a clenched fist. Life lived like this can get pretty tense. Two thousand million aspirin were sold in 1991 in the United Kingdom alone.

Our consciousness, however, is in every cell of our body. We give ourselves a lot more room in life when we begin to view our body in this way, and listen to its sensations and messages with the same regard we give our thoughts and feelings. We are even likely to find that our sensations come closer to the truth. To listen to the body, we need to value it, and consider it worth our attention. In the longer term, that may require us to look more closely and honestly into the attitudes and drives that motivate our behaviour; but even taking the time to register our bodily signals and act on them is a significant step towards a more erotic life.

Yesterday evening, I went to the Arnolfini, in Bristol, to have carrot and thyme soup with garlic bread. Only two mouthfuls had slipped down when I had the thought that nothing could be better than this. But then, halfway through the soup, I began thinking about dessert. Not any dessert, just a fudge brownie with ice-cream and hot chocolate sauce. They don't serve that at the Arnolfini, but I knew where they did. Park's, in Park Street, just up the road. And it's so much more pleasant there, anyway. There's no loud music playing, and they have a no-smoking area. It took me no time at all to convince myself. I finished my soup rather quickly, made straight for my car, and headed in the direction of Park Street. It was the time gap that gave me the break I needed to sense my true situation. I realized that I felt quite full. Faint gurglings were rising from my stomach. With the time to notice, I could feel I was already satisfied. It was just that my mind, as minds do, had run on to the next thing before finishing the first. This time, because of those few moments of grace in the car, the chain of desire was broken.

It wasn't that there was something wrong with chocolate

fudge brownies. On the contrary, I go along with my father's vernacular rendering of the middle way: he always used to say that a little bit of what you fancy does you good. He died at eighty-five, lean and strong, without having had a day's illness in his life. He loved white bread, jellied eels, and lardy cake. That's not all he ate, but that's what he loved, and he would have one or other of them from time to time. I wouldn't necessarily recommend his diet, and I certainly wouldn't follow it myself. But he always ate without eating too much, and he always enjoyed himself at the table. What we eat matters, but how much we eat, and the state of mind in which we eat, matters as much, if not more.

I drew level with Park's and slowed to a halt. The front of the restaurant is all glass, and I could see that only one table was occupied. It would be quiet in there, perfect for savouring the end of the day. It would be quieter in my own room, though, with its view over the chimneypots and the hills. My body felt alive and good just as it was. Whatever my mind might say, and however good fudge brownies are, anything more would have taken the edge off my senses. I drove home, and left dessert for another day.

*C*APPUCCINO

There are some pleasures which take on a distinctly original flavour when enjoyed alone. One of those, for me, is the breakfast *cappuccino*, downed before anyone else has reached the kitchen. I make it myself, me and my *cappuccino* machine, a regular morning exercise, a ritual of pure pleasure, every gesture a vital ingredient. Switch on, screw off the black hubcap and fill the belly of the machine with filtered water (coffee is my chosen poison, not tap water). Screw back the cap and grind some fresh Sumatran. Let the aroma curl round your nose. Fill the coffee container, swivel into position, and wait.

Those three or four minutes of waiting, that's when we begin to savour each other. The coffee knows I am there, flitting about with an eye on it, and it distils my anticipation into the brew. Whatever I busy myself with for that gap in time, the taste of what is to come is already on my tongue. Of course, I could give it up any time; but like any addict, I don't see the point. How delicious the waiting is, bittersweet.

When she starts to hiss, I know it's time, and I turn the knob that lets the dark juice flow, thick and pungent, into the cup. The cup matters. A *cappuccino* needs the right cup. It needs to be large and wide, almost a small bowl. In fact, sometimes a bowl will do perfectly. If it's a cup, a stout one works best, like the thick green china ones they use in France, the ones with corners, octagonal, I think. Then, it's good for the cup to have quite a thick lip, to hold the froth even when the liquid is right up to the edge.

So the water squeezes through the pulverized beans and into the light of day, black nectar now, with a hint of venom, a sting in its tail. But I like to hide its bite in frothing white milk. It is seething already in its jug under the steamer, that long silver spout which breathes like a dragon and drowns for a few seconds every other sound in the day. I withdraw the cup with its shiny black syrup, fill it to the brim with fluffiness and bubbles, and now a *cappuccino* puffs up, all white with brown veins, the lips smacking already and savouring the swell of it.

With two hands I take it, like a fateful draught in some rare chalice, and we become one body, the *cappuccino* and I. My innards are warmed with the strong comfort of it, the poison slips into my veins, my eyes lurch a little in their sockets and swivel to 'on'. Can this be real pleasure, or its imitation, indulgence? No, a second cup would be going too far, but there is no mistake, this is the real thing. Perhaps the hint of poison even adds to the pleasure. The Japanese certainly think so. One of their favourite dishes is the puffer fish, a species with a potent poison that carries off a stream of unfortunates every year from Tokyo's restaurants. But no, I like to think that my *cappuccino* is more akin to the tea ceremony than to a plate of puffer: it is a morning meditation with a difference. A Zen master, and everyone else who knows better, will see it another way, and smile.

THE BREAKFAST CLUB

The best breakfast restaurant I have ever been in was Joey's in San Francisco, at the Union Square end of Market. Joey was always there himself, behind the counter, with his blue-and-white-striped vest and thick, heavy arms bare from just above the elbows down, doing his hundredth over-easy of the morning and serving endless waffles and muffins – blueberry ones, or cinnamon, mostly – and sour cream and bagels if you wanted it, though I never did. It wasn't the breakfast I went there for – I usually had eggs scrambled on a muffin, and sometimes a slice of melon, which you could get anywhere downtown. No, I went there for the scene.

Joey's place was pure theatre, full of soul, with half a dozen different plays going on at once. It was one of those places that manages to defy cultural distinctions and fling the most unlikely people together at eight o'clock in the morning. The A & M (Acquisitions and Mergers) men were there most days. They looked like A & M people to me, anyway, the kind of people I have read about in the pages of Tom Wolfe's New York novel, *Bonfire of the Vanities*. Sharp suits, fine shirts, slim leather cases by their sides. Or perhaps they were property men, or film producers. They definitely did deals, whoever they were; deals involving serious money, other people's, most likely. They had the soft tones of men who charm their way along in life with the assistance of discreet and expensive aftershave.

I liked them, though; the way they leant over the table in turn with a sudden urgency and shuffled papers importantly, then laughed unexpectedly with heads thrown back and carefully styled haircuts blowing in Joey's overhead fans. Perhaps they liked Joey's gold pine tables and sleek cutlery, or just the sheer range of his menu. More likely, they just loved the feel of the place, as I did; or maybe the sense that they were out on the edge a little in here, in Joey's smart but somewhat funky café, a pleasant change from the smooth and sophisticated world that awaited them round the corner in some glitzy office off Union Square.

Joey's was a place for artists, for thinkers, philosophers, travellers, gays, Buddhists, and many of the other originals who still contribute to the spirit of that wonderful city. There was always the feeling that in Joey's you were in the middle of things, with a finger on the pulse of the city, without being anywhere slick. The clear and simple magnolia walls were hung with large framed prints each depicting in coloured paintings the attributes of a particular food – *Bread, The Potato, The Beetroot* – while the floor was glowing pine, varnished in gloss to bring out the best of the grain. Its unpretentiousness was part of Joey's appeal. So was the consideration that it was more cheap than expensive.

Billy was always there. Incongruously, he seemed always to be perched at the next table to the city slicks, a curious contrast to their careful elegance with his crumpled grey jacket, his torn and dirty jeans, and a T-shirt that said 'One For The Rollers'; though once I saw him in another one, yellow, with 'Go Slow' written across it. I think Joey looked after Billy. I mean, Billy never went short on breakfast, two eggs always over-easy, usually with ham. Ten dollars six days a week is a lot, and I'm sure Billy never had a regular job. Perhaps Joey's breakfast was his only meal of the day. Perhaps Joey owed him something from an earlier chapter in life.

Perhaps. But just as likely, those free breakfasts were simply one of Joey's contributions to the neighbourhood. It was one of those areas of the city which brought the chic and the street people up to the same corner, and in that way Joey's was a café of the people. He seemed to like it that way. He treated everyone as if they were an honoured guest – not by saying anything much, which would have been out of character, but with a welcome that was less decipherable by the eyes or the ears than by the body. You walked into Joey's and you *felt* welcome. You felt as if you counted, that the place acknowledged your presence. And somehow, this feeling had its origins with Joey. It was in those large brown eyes, which seemed to meet and acknowledge everyone who came through the door. It was in the thick shoulders and in the strong square hands; it was in the way he flipped the eggs and shook coarse black pepper over your plate till you asked him to stop. It was in the simple, repetitive actions that could be found in any breakfast restaurant in America. It was just that Joey did them differently. They were not a chore for him; nor were they a suave and efficient performance. He simply did them for you. That was it. He really made breakfast for *you*. He had two boys in white aprons who helped with the cooking, and he would come round and serve you himself.

He loved to stand over the chess players whenever he had the time. Joey's was quite a magnet for chess players. There would usually be a couple of games going, sometimes with Arthur playing two opponents at once. Arthur was from Boston, a young man in his twenties. He survived by his chess, with people paying a dollar to play him and giving him five dollars when he won. It was rarely a matter of 'if' – Arthur nearly always won. He would be there most mornings till noon, paying his dues with a coffee on the hour. Joey didn't mind. He seemed to like the kid, with his serious gaze, his lips usually gripped together tightly in a state of concern, fingers tapping the table quietly.

People in the neighbourhood knew of Arthur and would come to Joey's if they felt they could challenge him. Some of the tourists would try their luck, too. There was often a tourist or two in Joey's – not the package Japanese or midwest farmer's tour, but the single traveller or couple, usually quite young and from the East coast, or sometimes Europe. It was a men's café, predominantly; not by any design of Joey's, I'm sure, although his life didn't seem to have many women in it. He had no family of his own and, to my knowledge, only one brother, which was perhaps why he treated his clientele as family. Women came into Joey's, of course, but the tone was generally set by the low hum of male voices talking in a steady cadence, broken only by the sporadic laughter of the A & M men.

It was at the chess player's table that the accident happened. One day, despite years of steady practice, Joey slipped on a piece of tomato that had gone undetected on his polished pine floor. He fell heavily, and hit his temple against the corner of the chess player's table. He slumped to the floor in a heap. I was there when it happened. The whole place froze for an instant. There was nobody playing chess at the time, and Billy and the A & M men rushed to his aid while one of the cooks phoned for an ambulance. We heard the next day that Joey was still unconscious, and that it was feared he had a clot on the brain. By the end of the week, he was dead.

Most of the regulars turned out for the funeral. Arthur and I read appreciations, and everyone came back to the restaurant afterwards to share a brunch prepared by Joey's assistants and his brother, who had come in from Ohio. There was a woman helping them too, someone I had never seen before. Eggs Benedict, and half a dozen different breads. Dark bread with walnuts, unbleached bread with olives, raisin bread, and black Russian bread. These were Joey's favourites that he would add to the menu at weekends. Arthur told me later that he had heard that the woman had been the love of Joey's life thirty years before, and that though circumstances had made it impossible for them to come together, they had corresponded all that time.

Three months later the restaurant had been sold to a newcomer. He kept the same assistant cooks. He had the same menu, all but a few minor changes. He even kept the same name. Somehow, though, the food just didn't taste the same. Gradually the regulars drifted away, starting with Billy, and ending with me. Eventually, I understood. For all those mornings, Joey had fed us with himself. We had tasted of Joey's essence round those square wooden tables, and with his departure the place had lost its savour. The last time I passed by there, the placed was closed up. Only the name remained.

A Leisurely Lunch

Chloe is the woman I share my life with. One hot lunchtime, we went to an unassuming restaurant in a small village on the Montagne Noir, to the north of Carcassonne. It was a Sunday. Inside, the room was packed with French families. The French love to eat out *en famille*, especially on Sundays. The restaurant clung to the edge of a great gorge on which the village hung, and from the large plate window you could gaze out over the dizzy drop and see the crumbling Cathar tower sticking out of the twisted oaks like a melting wax finger. The place had the feeling of a private house more than a restaurant. To reach the dining room, you had to walk through what seemed to be a sitting room, complete with grandfather clock and three-piece suite. The half-dozen

SOUL AND SENSUALITY

tables in the dining room were full and, with a rare enthusiasm, the proprietor urged us to sit at the table in the
street. We were the only tourists, this area of France being
off the main routes, and the village had been left undis-
turbed by contemporary styles and affectations. Lunch was
a set menu, the table was shaded by a large white parasol,
and the street was silent. We sat down, returning his smile.

Within a few moments he came running out with a huge
bowl of coarse *pâté de campagne* held in a tight crust of butter.
He set it between us with two formidable knives and some
thick bread. He had two of these bowls, and they were
passed from table to table as people came and went, though
not many went. In the course of time, we gradually came to
understand why. We were encouraged to eat our fill and
help it down with the *cocktail de maison*, a sparkling wine
with real peach essence, far more fruity and with more bite
than the poor imitation to be found in English supermarkets.

In the shade of the parasol we sat and watched the
fountain play and the bees swarming over the yellow roses
climbing along the wall opposite our table. Only a dog
passed by in half an hour. Everyone else seemed to be in the
restaurant, and no one showed any sign of intending to
leave. This was Sunday lunch in France. We nattered con-
tentedly for a while, taking more of the pâté than we
normally would, in the absence of the appearance of any
thing else. The time inevitably came round when I could no
longer resist looking at my watch. We had been there for

almost an hour already, and there was still no sign that anything was ever going to replace the pâté. Neither was there any sign of the *patron*. I went in to find him, and he seemed a little taken aback. What was the matter? He looked at me with a mixture of embarrassment and incomprehension. Then he ran into the kitchen and came out with two more glasses of cocktail. *'Compliments de la maison!'* he smiled proudly.

It was another full half-hour before the *confit de canard* arrived. In that half-hour, we watched the dog scratch his ear with his hindleg, laughing at his acrobatic attempts to rid himself of his worst enemy; we wondered about the honeyed stone wall opposite, how long it had been standing, and the *lavoir* a few yards up the street, when women had last gathered there under its red tiled roof to chatter and to rub and scrub their men's working clothes clean. We wondered, as we always did, whether we would live in the region one day; and every now and then, we wondered – I more than Chloe – whether we should remonstrate any further about our fugitive *canard*.

When it came, stewed in its own juices, the most tender and delicate meat I have ever eaten, I felt as if I had been delivered into heaven. All my concerns and indignation evaporated in the first flush of its fragrance, and time simply ceased to exist. Softened in body and mind by the sun, the cocktails and the heavy pâté, warmed by the generosity of the portion, everything conspired to make us move slowly, each succulent mouthful interspersed with glances and grunts of approval and delight, with long looks at the roses, the stone, and each other, everything entering our mouths in unison on the end of the fork.

As my duck began to disappear from my plate, I began to feel gratitude for the patron's complete lack of airs, his lack of concern for my foreign haste, his instinctive capacity to serve food exactly as generations of men and women had done in that land before him. This leg of duck falling away from its bone, its recipe had stood the test of decades of discerning French palates. And now we, who had dropped in from another world, were the benefactors of all that distilled knowledge and enjoyment.

When we finally embarked upon the sorbet dessert, it was just after four; but I found it difficult to remember an afternoon more fruitfully spent. The patron came out to join us for a final *digestif*, happy with his labours and the results on our faces, and I thanked him for helping me learn to savour the passing of the hours.

The Flavour of a Place

It is a fine thing, to taste the salt of sea air on the tongue while walking the cliff path round the Lizard, in Cornwall. The air mixes with the ferns, whose spores leave a trace around the mouth and nose of dank, primeval forests, preserved now in layers of black humus, the distillation of a million years of life. Below on the rocks the English Channel spumes, throwing a light veil over the lower reaches of the path and a sheen over the face. Land such as this releases a richness into the air that feeds body and soul as surely as a three-course meal. We feed, literally, not just on food, but on all the torrents of impressions that pour through our senses daily. Few of these sustain us more than the impact of a special piece of land, its rocks, its earth, its plants and water.

The Russian mathametician and philosopher, P.D. Ouspensky, said that

> with every external impression, whether it takes the form of sound, or vision, or smell, we receive from outside a certain amount of energy, a certain number of vibrations; this energy which enters the organism from outside is food. Moreover, energy cannot be transmitted without matter. If an external impression brings external energy with it into the organism, it means that external matter enters which feeds the organism in the full meaning of the term.[3]

There are places in this world that are known to feed us more than most. Some of them have been revered as holy sites for centuries. One such place, where I once went walking, is Mount Athos, a finger of land that sticks out some ten miles into the northern Aegean from mainland Greece. There are twenty-one Orthodox monasteries on Athos, most of which have been there for several hundred years or more.

The whole peninsula has been sacrosanct for almost two thousand years, since the time, it is said, that the Virgin Mary was shipwrecked there and saved from a terrible storm. From then on, Athos was considered the earthly realm of Mary, and access to it has been forbidden to all other women ever since.

I went there for two weeks in 1974, and walked along the footpaths (there are no roads) from monastery to monastery, a guest of the brethren. I would walk all day and arrive in the late afternoon at the gates of a monastery, usually to be greeted by the guestmaster with the traditional glass of schnapps. I often walked, or rather scrambled, over the cliff paths hanging precariously over steep drops of shale that plunged into the dazzling azure below; through forests where the path would peter out and leave me turning in circles; up steep crags and rocky bluffs where everything was sky, a vast canopy of blue; and through sheaves of white and silver light. When I reached the monastery in the evening, I was always surprised to notice how little food I wanted. A bowl of thin soup and a slice of bread filled me up till morning, when I would take another slice of bread with thick black coffee. I would never have lunch, and yet my body, my being, was humming at a finer, faster rate, that I have only rarely reached again since. Suddenly, one morning on the path above the ocean, I realized what it was: I was being fed, literally filled up, with the wind, the water, the hard earth, the slant of Greek light, and the vibrations of tens of thousands of monks who had lived out their lives on this land in an intensity of prayer.

There are less rarified foods than prayer, however, which a body like mine can enjoy. Bath, in England, has always had a flavour as libertarian as Athos is puritan. It is hard to imagine penance of any kind taking place here, in this most sensuous city in all England. England is hardly renowned for its love of the senses, but if you had to sniff out the most sensuous city there is in that country, you would certainly end up in Bath. No sharp cut of thyme or rosemary here among the rocks to slice through my daydreams; no, Bath is a city where I go to be soothed, softened, and sweetened. It is the honey colour of the soft limestone that gives it such a sweet taste. The soft curve of its crescents, like the Royal Crescent, lulls visitor and inhabitant alike into a slower pace than the straight avenues of faster, more modern cities.

Under the city the warm, healing waters of Minerva[4] swell. It is they who leave a heaviness lingering in the late afternoon air. I prefer the water's smell on the wind to its tangible presence in a cup. When I lived in Bath, from the age of seven to eighteen, there was a fountain outside the Roman Baths with a bronze cup attached to it by a chain. My mother always used to encourage me to taste Minerva's waters there, straight from the source, and I gagged on it every time. Perhaps it was the tepid temperature of it, or more likely the abundance of minerals that were meant to be so good for me; or even, perhaps, the metal of the tarnished cup, lifted by so many hopeful hands already. I didn't like it, anyway, and I usually managed to obliterate its taste (and its goodness) with a banana milkshake in Hand's Dairy across the street.

Bath is sweet, even so; sweet with the indulgence of more than two hundred years of ladies and gentlemen of a certain distinction who came here for the pleasure of each other's company, and for the cure by those very same waters that I used to retch upon. It remains even now a slow city of leisure, for strolling in, and its mellow air seeped deep into my bones during the years of life in which we are all most susceptible to impressions. With all the strolling I have done in its streets, with the hours I have spent sitting on its lawns, in its teashops and squares, looking up at its soberly beautiful buildings and gazing across its river Avon to Sham Castle on the horizon, it must have ingested as much of me down through the years as I have of it. I am spread out through its streets in the same way that it lives in my body. For in a love that is real, we are consumed by places and people in the exact degree that we take them into ourselves.

It is probably because of an excess of honey from a youth spent in Bath that I hanker periodically for rock and desert and the hot fire of a far southern sun. After only the first day in the Sahara I feel myself drying out and being reduced to the lean essentials of bleached bone and tightened skin. In the desert, I breathe iron into my soul. My blood is thinned, my mucuses dried, my thoughts are sharpened and separated by gaps of glistening silence. Into that silence the light pours down and fills me until there is no place left to hide, just me and the endless expanse of sun and sand moving in and out of each other in a ceaseless exchange of elements.

EATING WORDS

Sex is good, but not as good as fresh sweet corn.   **Garrison Keillor**

Wine is sure proof that God loves us and wants us to be happy.   **Benjamin Franklin**

How simple and frugal a thing is happiness – a glass of wine, a roast chestnut, a wretched little brazier, the sound of the sea . . .   **Nikos Kazantzakis**

It requires a certain kind of mind to see beauty in a hamburger bun.   **Ray Kroc**

No mean woman can cook well, for it calls for a light head, a generous spirit, and a large heart.
Paul Gauguin

Too few people understand a really good sandwich.
James Beard

There is more simplicity in the man who eats caviar on impulse than in the man who eats grapenuts on principle.
G.K. Chesterton

To as great a degree as sexuality, food is inseparable from imagination.   **Jean François Revel**

After a good dinner one can forgive anybody, even one's own relations.   **Oscar Wilde**

Cooking is love. It should be entered into with abandon or not at all.   **Harriet Van Horne**

Never eat more than you can lift.   **Miss Piggy**

Wine brings to light the hidden secrets of the soul.
Horace, *Epistles*

One barrel of wine can work more miracles than a church full of saints.   **Italian proverb**

All from Michael Cader's book, *Eat These Words*, except for the last three quotes, which were found in *The Wine Quotation Book* ed. Jennifer Taylor.

$\mathcal{F}$EEDING ON $\mathcal{A}$IR

I have never known anyone speak about the pleasure of breathing with such obvious delight as Thich Nhat Hanh,[5] the Buddhist monk who headed the local effort to care for the dying and wounded in Saigon during the Vietnam War. His advice then to the thousands of monks and lay helpers under his guidance was to pick up the broken bodies while continuing to breathe deeply from the belly. Why would he suggest such a thing? Their attentiveness to their own breathing gave them an anchor in the extreme circumstances under which they were working. It helped them not to get swept away by their own or others' emotional distress. But there was another reason: breathing is our most direct connection with everything else that lives and breathes, since the same air passes in and out of everyone's lungs. In asking his monks to breathe with attention, he was asking them to become sensitive to the undying current that passes through victim, persecutor and helper, and that unites them all in the ceaseless round of life and death. Through an attentiveness to their breath, the monks were practising compassion.

Bringing attention to the fact of our breathing – not changing it, or doing anything about it, but simply being aware of the process – brings us into contact not only with others and the surrounding environment, it also forges a deeper connection with ourselves, and with the intrinsic pleasure of being alive. I sit here listening to Tai, as he is known, speaking about the enjoyment of following the rise and fall of the breath and I wonder whether he is not stretching a point. After all, I have been breathing for a long time now without being aware of any special pleasure or pain. It is difficult to imagine how an automatic activity should suddenly become enjoyable other than through the power of suggestion.

But I let my attention follow my breath down from the tip of my nose to the depths of my belly and up again. My nostrils feel the cool stream, my chest rises to accommodate the downflow of life, freely given, and passes it on down to my belly, warming it on the way. Over the next few breaths I notice old passions stir; a fleeting face crosses my mind, mountains tingle in an imagined distance, and half a dozen breaths slip by without my noticing. I leave my attention in the belly, a little above the navel, and let the breath take care of itself, drawing the life into me in its own rhythm and time. The passage of air moves through my inner cavities and slows down, waiting for an instant between one breath and the next, leaving me in the widening gap between one thought and the next.

Sitting here, in the circle of breath, I see how the lungs are the motor of thought; how the subtler the breath, the subtler the thought, and how in the gap between breaths all thought fades away like a ripple from the surface of a pond. The breath passing through me now is barely discernible from the air that moves around my skin and the rest of the room in barely perceptible currents. Rising and falling, in and out it goes, reaching down into me like a slender thread fishing in my darkest reaches for some unsuspecting memory or feeling, which, however, fails to rise now and disturb this most intimate exchange between whoever I am and whatever the world is.

Feeding on air – this Buddhist monk is right: the passage of air through the body is an exquisite sensation which, if followed for a while with a steady gaze, gathers the person into a nourishing silence. Being breathed in this way - for no effort is involved – is a quiet joy, the joy of life streaming through all things and imparting its essence with a generosity impervious to rank or station. This, I see now, is why Tai asked his monks to abide in their breathing while carrying the dead and wounded of Saigon. The breath of the departed feeds us even now, and remembering our own breathing takes us beyond the pleasures and pains of the passing moment to an enduring sense of union with all things through time.

THE FAMILY LUNCH

I shall never forget those peas, bright green ones, frozen, I think, served from an oval perspex bowl. They would always roll around my plate in a brief moment of abandon before my mother cornered them with a serving of roast potatoes and three slices of lamb oozing with gravy. Even the words on the paper make my nose wrinkle now in disbelief that I could have digested so many of those Sunday roasts, and even with a certain relish, all those years ago. Now it would be asparagus, or *mangetout*, with brown rice or fish, accompanied by a glass of dry white wine. Then, a series of cups of tea would have washed it all down. Tastes change, and what is good or bad taste I know even less now than I did then.

I know there was something I enjoyed about those family lunches. It was to do with the plentifulness, with the gathering together, the opportunity for conversation, and with the brightness of the peas. I liked my brother's stories and my father's grunts of approval and his evident enjoyment of the meat. I liked the tangible satisfaction of my mother who once again had provided enough fare to settle half a dozen stomachs. I never did like the boiled cabbage, though, a habit my parents had brought with them from the war years. What I was really there for was the dessert. I have preferred apple crumble and cream to almost any other dessert ever since. I read somewhere that love of the food of one's childhood is a form of patriotism. I think I know what that means. Apple crumble and cream, even now, merge into a jumbled sensation of security and warmth which gathers to it a sense not only of family but of place. In my case, England. I could never imagine eating apple crumble in Provence, or Los Angeles. If I were asked whether patriotism played any part in my life today, I would laugh and say I am a European and, secondly, a citizen of the world. But I have to admit that my mother's dessert, and the place of its origin with which it is indissolubly united in my mind, still holds a corner of my heart for itself alone. Of all the dishes that she placed before me, that is the one that still delights me today.

My father would always sit next to the door, and would start as soon as his plate was laid before him. Having spoken little, being wholly absorbed in the delight on the end of his fork, and never eating large portions, he would usually finish before everyone else. Then, with a deferring look to my mother, he would ease himself out of the room before dessert to read the paper next door. The rest of us would sit round the crumble, eaten always from blue bowls with little white flowers running round the outside rim, with large spoons tarnished in the middle from such regular usage. My mother had arthritis and was careful in her diet, but a teaspoon of thick cream and a thimbleful of crumble was her permitted excess. It was then, towards the end of the meal, that the talking would take over, fuelled by the engine of my mother's desire for conversation which, she said, along with laughter, always helps the digestion. We would talk about nothing in particular, the current news, some local gossip, a book someone had just read, the ordinary paraphernalia of family affairs. We talked small talk, but in those exchanges the warmth of belonging was passed between us with a steadiness that rests with me even now.

Once, not so long ago, the talk grew larger around that same table. It was the day after my father died. Never was his presence felt so much as on that day. It was the lunch that brought our private mournings together in one place. His seat was empty, but we laid it anyway, in honour of one who had sat with us all those years and sustained us with his quiet and steady being. My mother was quieter than usual, of course, without her bustle, but when she spoke her words fell straight from her heart. She had lived her whole life with this man who was suddenly not there. At eighty-five his heart had decided to stop beating. She told us how she had never looked at another man from the moment she met him, some fifty years earlier; of the happiness they shared in their ordinary, uneventful lives; of the uncanny sense she had of his presence, even though his body was no longer there. Over the peas and potatoes, I told her and my sister how, only the week before, after I had taken my parents for tea in a country hotel, he had murmured a few words which, for all their apparent insignificance, were a deliberate statement of love: 'Mind how you go, now, we can't have anything happening to you.' I had smiled at the time, and put my arm round his shoulder, knowing he was expressing his love in the best way he could. I had felt in that instant that he was saying goodbye to me, and that when his death came we had already completed our affairs for this lifetime. I told them this over lunch, and how his passing for me felt like the falling of a ripe apple from his tree in the garden. It was with apples from that tree that my mother made the crumble that day.

$\mathscr{T}$ANGERINE $\mathscr{D}$REAM

I once dreamed I was sitting under a rock in the desert, surrounded by red sand that stretched to a glittering haze on the horizon. I had a goatskin which was still half-full of water, but I had just run out of my last tin of food the night before. I was aware that my situation did not appear promising, but I was not, for some reason, especially concerned. I gazed for a long while out at the ocean of sand, and felt its stillness quieten my mind. There was not a breath of wind, only a roaring sunlight and the metre of shade from my rock.

As I was looking out over the desert, I was astounded to see a little out of arm's reach, over to my left, a bright tangerine perched on the sand, I had brought no tangerines into the desert. No one else could have passed this way recently. There were no tyre tracks or footmarks. Yet there it was, all by itself, a bulging tangerine, perfectly round, a meal for one in an orange suit. I leaned over and picked it up. It smelled fresh and bright, as tangerines do. I felt its soft mandarin skin and cracked it open like a ripe pod to reveal the fruit and its protection of sinewy latticework. It released a cool mist of delicious odour into the desert air and over my hot face.

With my index finger I slowly pulled one of the segments away and brought it, trailing a rubbery white frond, to the edge of my lips. Holding it for a moment between my teeth, I eventually split the tight skin and a shower of fine juices sprayed into my mouth. Slowly, I chewed the flesh out of the segment, reduced it to pulp, and let it slip effortlessly down my throat with barely the reflex of swallowing. I savoured its energy, and felt it clear my head. Then I tore off another segment, full to bursting, felt its body billowing between my fingers, and sent it the same way as its absent neighbour. A third and fourth segment followed, then another, and another; the cool shock of their tang travelled right through me until, with the last one, I awoke to a cool autumn morning in England.

Dinner for Two

In late April, some years ago now, Chloe invited me to dinner in her apartment. She had placed a tall white candle in the middle of her square oak table and laid two white plates opposite each other. It was the first time one of us had made dinner for the other. We had been to restaurants together, we had made love already, we had been friends from the moment we met. But we had never sat down at the other's table. She lived in a garden flat at the time, with little light at the end of the day. At seven, when she opened the door to me, her corner lights were on, giving a soft, dim glow and leaving large shafts of shadow across the middle of the room. She was in a marvellous evening dress of royal blue silk which hung from a halter neck down to her ankles. She looked gorgeous, and it was her I wanted to eat, never mind the meal.

As I stepped through her door, though, I suddenly felt shy. Chloe, too, seemed unusually self-conscious, she who was normally so abandoned and laughing, head tossed back with a barely concealed wildness. We sat for a while on her sofa, wine glass in hand, and our talking, slow and some-what measured, continued over the occasional leaps she made to the stove to stir and hover over her creations.

She eventually lit the candle on the table and ushered me to the seat furthest from the stove. She placed two bowls of soup, steaming mushroom and ginger, down at our places, and sat opposite me with a smile and a sense of finality. On its way over to reach for the bread my arm slowed with the realization that a strange gravity had fallen upon us. We looked at each other across the table. We stayed there for what felt like minutes on end, my hand clutching its bread, the steam on the soup dying away, our lips falling silent. I felt rooted to the chair, and the air between us was so thick with unspoken words that it felt ready to burst.

It struck us both at the same time that we had fallen into a ritual that was enacted all over the world. Since the beginning of time, in straw huts, in smart London apartments, in homes across every continent, women had sat down at table with men with whom they shared their lives. That night, for some reason, the act of Chloe serving me food had cast us as husband and wife, and the husbands and wives of all time were standing behind our chairs, slotting us into their roles. It felt, too, as if we ourselves had been together for aeons, and this was the latest of countless meals we had eaten in each other's company.

'The soup's best eaten hot,' Chloe said. I took my bread in both hands and broke it in two, the soft white dough moulding to the imprint of my fingers. I dipped it in the soup and brought it to my mouth, the mushroom and ginger vying for appreciation on the edges of my tongue. Slowly, the gravity lifted away, and we were two lovers again having dinner together by candlelight. I watched her long, delicate fingers picking her bread apart with an almost fragile grace, and wondered at the universe of hands, how her hand could be so different to my own. Eating her soup, I took in as well her visit to the grocer's that afternoon, her picking out of the mushrooms and her slicing of the ginger later on over the stove. I breathed in her warmth in the last strains of steam that rose from my bowl when I stirred the contents with my spoon.

She had enjoyed laying this table, I could feel it. It was in the considered yet carefree arrangement that had conspired to bring beauty to this simple, shady room in the basement of a Georgian house in Bristol. She rose to fetch the wine, a dry Sauvignon from Australia in a bottle tinted lightly with green. As she returned to fill our glasses the candlelight caught the blue of her dress and threw its purple shadow into the wine. We raised our glasses and drank to each other. Then we spoke of little things and basked in long silences. What words were spoken slipped between us like silver fish down waterfalls.

Chloe eventually cleared the soup bowls and replaced them with thick dinner plates from Mexico, handpainted in the middle with purple grapes and light blue flowers. On to my plate she laid a portion of wild salmon which had been poached in bay leaves; *mangetout* cooked lightly in butter and a spoonful of basmati rice. We sat for a moment, contemplating her creation, and then I followed her lead and brought the first taste of salmon to my mouth. Her tongue curled slowly out of her mouth to lick the juice of the fish from her unpainted lips, and I fancied that in that lick she was tasting not only the salmon but me as well, fishing me in from across the table. I wondered what flavour I was. I knew the taste of Chloe: firm ripe peaches with the sweetness of milk.

The salmon fell away from its bone with a touch of the fork, and dissolved easily under the press of our teeth. My teeth slowed to follow her more leisurely pace, so that our meals could disappear more or less together, and when I did finish, it was only a couple of mouthfuls before her.

'I have never quite realized before tonight how we eat everything,' Chloe said. 'That is, if things are in the right place with each other. I feel we know each other from the inside in a way that could only happen like this. Not only each other, though; the room, the light, the salmon, the wine, all of it has passed into our bodies over this last hour or so and added a measure to who we are.'

$\mathcal{M}$ANGO

For dessert we had mango, and that night we fed it to each other. It was a ripe one, green skin turned to yellow and orange at either end. Chloe slit it open with a long, sharp knife, severing the two sides from the stone in the middle. Then she brought her chair round to my side of the table and held one of the slices out to me with both hands. I leant forward and sucked the golden juices and the soft striated flesh of the fruit. The odour of mango, sweet and heavy, went to my head as I turned the first mouthful over slowly with my tongue. Could there be any food carrying the signature of paradise more legibly than this? An indescribable sweetness tinged with just the right edge of asperity.

I moved to it again, deeper in this time, and the silky strands covered my lips and even my cheeks with a yellow sheen. Having food brought to one's mouth by another person is a close and intimate thing. It is even more sweet when the other is someone you love. A gratitude wells up with the first mouthful. How delicate we are, how prone to hurt and misunderstanding, there with our mouth open, defenceless as a babe, as the other brings a spoon to our lips laden with the sweetest of food. Being fed is a lesson in receiving. You get just as much as the other decides to put on the spoon, and you get it in their time, rather than your own. It certainly slows eating down.

I took the other side of the mango and began feeding it to her. I had never put so much food in anyone's mouth before, not a whole slice of mango, bite by bite. I began to feel what it was like to be of service to another person. I had not judged correctly when I was being fed myself: this was not something happening in Chloe's time, nor in mine, but in a time of its own, blended from a sensitivity to each other's pace. When she finished the first mouthful, I needed to sense when she was ready for the next, and the appropriate pace with which to deliver the fruit to her lips. It was as if she was eating for us both, and I could feel the taste of mango on my tongue as she moved it around in her mouth.

The evening slowed to the pace of a mouthful at a time, each one an event on its own which both of us could feel not only between the teeth and over the roof of the mouth but pervading the entire body. Our breathing rose and fell in the same rhythm, and held us to a still centre around which all these sensations flowed and moved between us. To have lost ourselves in the ecstasy of the tasting would have been a lesser joy than this; for in the stillness we spread out beyond the thrill of the body to bring down the moon into that yellow mango.

$\mathscr{A}$ $\mathscr{T}$ABLE FOR $\mathscr{O}$NE

I have just eaten breakfast alone, *cappuccino* and muesli, and I realize now that I don't remember a single mouthful. My mind was full of this and that, and all I remember is getting up from a bowl that was suddenly empty with a certain discomfort in my belly. I am reminded of a story by René Daumal in which he tells of a man who had longed for fresh kippers throughout the Second World War.[6] He finally sat down to the dish of his delight in 1946 with a friend he hadn't seen for some years. They talked animatedly until, at one moment, our friend looked down at his plate and saw that it was empty. He had gobbled down his dream without noticing it.

That is how I felt this morning on contemplating my empty bowl. Conversation can kill taste, although it can enhance it as well. Solitude is the same. Sometimes a solitary meal can be soured by loneliness. Especially in a restaurant and especially, a female friend has assured me, for women. I had never thought of it until Gabrielle[7] pointed it out. She travels a lot on her own, and often finds herself in a restaurant at a table for one. Even now, she says, in the 1990s, waiters will sometimes smirk at her with an attention that suggests she is looking for a man; couples at the other tables will break off their conversation every now and then to throw a glance her way. It seems there is still something weird, not quite right, about a woman dining alone; and especially, Gabrielle says, in an Italian restaurant.

I have felt something of the same as a man, though I suspect it derives from my own self-consciousness rather than from any social prejudice. Eating alone in a restaurant where everyone else is in company can make me acutely aware of my aloneness. The aloneness can, according to the time of day, the nature of the food, the mood of the moment, take a downward curve into loneliness. Perhaps that is why I gobbled my muesli this morning, to circumvent that downward emotion and replace it with a rapid, if uncomfortable, feeling of fullness. Another way I avoid what is occasionally the discomfort of being with myself is to be busy while eating my meal, as if the food were a necessary but irksome chore. I read a book, have newspapers around me, or a pen in my hand. I eat as if being alone means I don't matter, or the food doesn't matter, spooning mouthfuls out of tins and bits of toast and old cheese, as if I only existed through the eyes of other people.

Yet solitude is usually one of my great delights, and eating in my own company often a real pleasure. Housden sits down with Housden and gives him the time of day. He has the sense of his own presence, and the luxury of a meal – whatever it is – which can have his undivided attention. Eating alone is a gap in the day's busy-ness, a time for recollection, and for savouring the moment.

The most memorable meal I have ever had alone was in Mexico, early in January 1992. I was in southern Mexico looking for the rainforest. Go to San Cristóbal, they told me, up in the Chiapas Highlands. There you will find high altitude rainforest. I went to San Cristóbal on a battered old bus up tortuous bends that wound through the mountains. San Cristóbal de las Casas is a fine old colonial town hours from anywhere. It has a lot to offer: the Mother Earth Café, serving brown rice salads, granola, and chocolate brownies; a dozen arcades, full of antique shops and clothes stores, that would fit easily into Mill Valley or anywhere else along the more sophisticated Californian coastline; plenty of Chiapas Indians selling their beadwork, and hundreds of refugees from Western materialism who have fled there to the simple life. Except there are so many of them that it's not a whole lot simpler than Mill Valley, and almost as prosperous. All of this, none of which I was expecting, but no rainforest.

Go to the Montebello Lakes, on the Guatemalan border, about three hours away. There you will find rainforest. So I took another battered bus to the Lakes. They are very beautiful, empty of people, clear blue pools with the shadows of pine darkening their edges. Pine forest. Just like the Highlands of Scotland. I gave up on the rainforest for the day, though I was sure it must be in the area somewhere, and took the old bus back to town.

Only a few minutes had gone by when I saw a track on the left running off from the road and a sign,

'Museo-Parador'. I remembered that my friend in San Cristóbal had said this would be a good place to stay by the
Lakes. In a sudden change of direction, I shouted to the
driver to stop, clambered off the bus with my backpack and
began walking up the track into what seemed like the
middle of nowhere. It *was* the middle of nowhere. The track
ran up a slow incline for half a mile and then turned abruptly
to the right. At the bend there was another sign, reassuring
me that I was indeed on my way to the Museo-Parador,
though there was no sign of human habitation anywhere.
Another twenty minutes of tramping through dry scrub and
grasses and I was on the edge of a steep valley which
plunged to a lake below. On the other side a wooded slope
rose steeply to the sky. My path ran along the ledge to a
range of low buildings that had emerged on the lip of the
hill. Their red tiled roofs were just catching the last of the
afternoon sun as it trailed through the trees on the other side
of the lake.

It was the Museo-Parador. I walked through the
wrought-iron gate and stood in disbelief. In the middle of
this wild and empty landscape was one of the most beautiful
buildings I had ever seen. Just one man was there, swaying
backwards and forwards in a cane rocking-chair on the
verandah. Before him was a coarse grass lawn some eighty
yards deep which ended in a low perimeter wall. The man
rose to meet me with an outstretched arm. The Mexico of my
mind had already been dislodged by my experience of San

Cristóbal. If this was a Third World country, I was not sure what could be said about England. Mexico is enjoying an economic upsurge which is making the recession of its northern neighbour and Britain seem a highly local affair. Now my Mexican fantasy was about to be dealt another blow. The man who rose from the rocking-chair shook my hand and asked me if I would like to visit the Museo, which was the first of several rooms off the verandah. The door was open, and I could see that paintings were hung around the walls. There was not a single work by a Mexican artist. Instead, my eyes fell upon Victorian English landscapes, some French portraits of the same era, a genuine Goya, and a Picasso! Deep in the Chiapas Highlands, ten miles from Guatemala. The young man explained that he was a picture restorer, and that he was in partnership with a man from the local town (thirty miles away) who had returned from making his fortune in Europe. They had wanted to restore a colonial hacienda to its former glory in order to celebrate the traditional local architecture, which had been largely replaced in the area by concrete buildings. At the same time, they wanted to offer the region a small museum of European art. The owner had collected some works during his time in Europe, and this museum was furnished with those and with other works lent by friends. The ultimate whim, an eccentricity worthy of Oscar Wilde.

I walked back into the sunlight, no longer sure of where, or even who, I was. I was looking for the primeval wildness of a rainforest. How had I conspired to bring this place into my life? My eyes followed the verandah and its line of tapering pine columns down to an open dining room without walls but with a domed glass roof, not unlike a Victorian conservatory. A dozen tables were laid with white linen tablecloths. When I told the man, whose name was Alfonso Torreon, that I wanted to stay the night, he walked down the verandah and threw open the remaining six doors. Each room had its own European antique furniture, a four-poster bed in one, a Napoleonic clock in another, set amid bare white walls and a clay tile floor. Every room looked across the verandah to the wooded slope and the setting sun. Every room was vacant. All this beauty for just Alfonso, the cook, two gardeners, and me. The cost, twenty-five dollars a night. They were not open, Alfonso murmured gravely, for the purpose of profit. This was an affair of the heart. The hacienda had struck him and his partner alike as the perfect setting for their dream. They had laboured for months to make what I saw now, and they had only been open three weeks. They had stripped layers of paint off the wooden columns, each one a whole tree, they had built the conservatory, planted the lawn, and made a haven in the heart of the wildness.

I spent the rest of the day on the verandah in a wicker chair gazing out over the scene. Just before sunset an old lady appeared from nowhere with a basket of eggs, and urged Alfonso to buy some. He asked me what I would like for dinner. Eggs would be fine for breakfast, I answered. The old woman shuffled off happily into the dusk.

At seven-thirty I was sitting in solitary splendour beneath the glass dome with a view down the verandah, lit now with oil lamps swinging from the ceiling. Two oil lamps suspended from the glass dome gave a mellow light to my table for one, and the edge of civilization was marked by a row of flares that had been lit along the perimeter wall. Beneath the sound of the cicadas, the silence was deep and still. That night, I ate the silence; I ate guacamole with crisp tortillas, a corn soup tinged with chilli, I ate enchiladas, que-sadillas, and heartily enjoyed the pleasure of my own company. Alfonso served me at his leisure over the next hour and a half, and when I eventually rose from this fairy-tale table, it was with a profound gratitude for all eccentrics who dare to follow their dream. The rainforest, I decided, could wait. I would stay here another three days.

$\mathcal{S}$ MELLING

He would often just stand there, leaning against a wall or crouching in a dark corner, his eyes closed, his mouth half-open and nostrils flaring wide, quiet as a feeding pike in a great, dark, slowly moving current. And when at last a puff of air would toss a delicate thread of scent his way, he would lunge at it and not let go. Then he would smell at just this one odour, holding it tight, pulling it into himself and preserving it for all time. The odour might be an old acquaintance, or a variation on one; it could be a brand-new one as well . . . the odour of pressed silk, for example, the odour of wild-thyme tea, the odour of brocade embroidered with silver thread, the odour of cork from a bottle of vintage wine, the odour of a tortoiseshell comb.

Patrick Susskind, *Perfume* [1]

$\mathcal{S}$MELL $\mathcal{M}$EMORIES

butter in the dish on a warm day

the mustiness of my parents' living room

mock-orange blossom in a country garden

honeysuckle in a hedge

hashish in a Moroccan tearoom

piss, the stale reek of it, in a London urinal

clover honey

a ripe banana, just peeled

clean sheets on the line

seaweed washed up on the beach

burning hoof in a blacksmith's

the tangled skein of spices in an Indian meal

the smell of polish in my headmaster's study

my father's pipe tobacco, Dutch aromatic

petrol, when I overfilled the tank

fresh rain on summer fields

fresh-ground coffee beans

rosemary and thyme in Provence

my lover's arms and shoulders

a burning sage-stick

undergrowth in the woods after a downpour

hot chocolate made with milk

$\mathscr{F}$OLLOWING OUR $\mathscr{N}$OSES

Of all our senses, smell is the most primal; it is also the most pervasive, insubstantial and difficult to verbalize. Smell is primitive; as primitive as the tick who waits on the branch of a tree somewhere in South America, curled in a ball, giving nothing to the world, not even the tiniest drop of perspiration. Blind, dumb, deaf, it does nothing but sniff; it sniffs for months on end for the blood of some passing animal and then drops – its only movement – on to the unsuspecting host, into whose flesh it instantly bores.[2] When we humans were just beginning to move from the world of the four-leggeds to the precarious posture of the biped, it was the smell on the wind and in the grasses, as much as our eyes or ears, that would bring news of food, foe and the mating season. The olfactory bulb is in the early brain, connected with our earliest racial and personal memories; it has little to say to the frontal lobes, which house the motor of language.

It is difficult to describe smell precisely because the odours of the world seep directly into the most archaic regions of the brain, without the filter of the conscious mind. When the olfactory bulb is fired by a signal it sends a message straight to the limbic system, the seat of primal emotion. Its relations are especially intimate with that first urge, the call of the opposite sex. Because smells are so closely connected with emotion, and have only a tenuous link with reason, we try and describe them less by their particular properties than by how they make us feel.[3] They are delightful, sickening, revolting, or intoxicating. With our eyes closed and our preconceptions lifted, we jumble them up and find it difficult to distinguish orange from rose. A family I know once played the blindfold game of guessing which things were on a tray from their smell. When the daughter smelled her stepfather's socks, famous in the family for their sweaty stench, she identified them as rosewater. The stepfather always recalls the moment now whenever anyone complains of his feet.

We live in an ocean of smell, yet we usually move through its teeming eddies and currents as if we had no nose at all. Long gone are the fine nasal sensibilities of the tundra and savannah; for most of us, the nose is now little more than something to blow on. Yet everything that has enough volatility to release molecules into the air smells. The elements smell, people smell, animals and all vegetation smells. The world simmers in a stew of smell, and we take it into ourselves with every breath. Most of the time, we will say we do not smell anything. Radiological scanning techniques, however, show activity in the odour-related areas of the brain of a person who emphatically denies all awareness of any smell.[4]

Whether we know it or not, the world passes through us

and emerges altered. Through all our senses we transform the world, taking it in, turning it around, and letting it loose again, subtly different to what it was without us; while we in our turn are invisibly moulded and shaped by its passage. With smell and taste, this is not only a subtle but an obvious, physical exchange. We take smell in on the breath, and a breath is never neutral or bland; each one is cooked on our internal fire and sent back out into the world in a different chemical state to the way it came in. Somewhere in the cooking, between the in-breath and the out-breath, the smell enters the chemistry of the body, shifting our mood, perhaps, or our thoughts, without our even knowing it.

From the time we raised ourselves away from the scent trails of the ground to the full stature of two-legged existence, our sense of smell has progressively diminished in favour of eyes that could scan the horizon. Though we rely less now on odour than at any previous evolutionary stage, our sense of smell is still the most underrated of all the senses. The expression 'to be led by the nose' suggests that our instincts are unreliable and foolish; that reason alone should be the arbiter of our actions. Yet knowledge comes in many guises. Smells tell us of an atmosphere; they inform our deepest emotions and our loftiest aspirations; they determine, often against all reason, our attraction or aversion to others. Androsterone, a chemical cousin of testosterone, is the male essential oil.[5] It is said to smell approximately of musk, sandalwood, and a nuance of urine. There have been experiments that showed women selecting only the chairs, telephones, and theatre seats which had been pre-sprayed with androsterone.[6] The most alluring fragrance in a woman occurs at ovulation. The apparent 'sweetness' of the breath at this time is enhanced by the rise in blood sugar level which occurs at ovulation.[7] Although sugar has no odour of its own, sweetness lifts all fragrance and renders it more attractive.

Then, apart from the odour of their gender, each individual has a scent which is as distinctive as their fingermark. It is unlikely that you find the odour of your partner distasteful, although we have become too distant from the natural odour of the body to be likely to appreciate the gift of a love apple. In Elizabethan times, women would put a peeled apple under their arm until it was full of their natural flavour. Then they would give it as a gift to their beloved. Even Napoleon asked Josephine not to wash in the two weeks before they would next meet, so he could enjoy her undiluted.

Alongside this time-honoured appreciation for the exhalations of nature, people of all cultures have taken pleasure in anointing themselves with the perfumes of flowers, of spices, and animal secretions, since the beginning of recorded history. Ladies of the court in Pharaonic Egypt put tall wax cones of incense on their heads. The heat of the scalp would gradually melt the cone, washing each lady with fragrant oils as she moved about her day. In Nero's Rome, there were over a thousand baths that specialized in fragrances: *unctuaria*. The Incense Road, like the better-known Silk Road, was one of the world's busiest trade routes for centuries.

The priests and priestesses of all times and religions have known this well: that perfumes and incense can exalt the soul and add a spiritual dimension to this mortal existence. Egyptian records dating back to 4,500 B.C. tell of perfumed oils, scented barks and resins, spices, and aromatic vinegars, all used in medicine, ritual, and embalming. The temples were perfumed with crushed cedarwood bark, caraway seeds and angelica roots steeped in oils or burned (per-fume, with smoke). A favourite perfume was *kyphi*, a blend of sixteen different essences, including myrrh and juniper.[8] It was inhaled by Egyptian priests to heighten their spiritual receptivity. Rosewater and musk were mixed into the mortar of Islamic mosques, and the musk can still be detected today, hundreds of years later. Catholic and Orthodox churches still burn the plant resins of frankincense and myrrh, both of which were in use long before Christ's time. Herodotus (fifth century B.C.) mentions the delivery of thirty tons of frankincense to the king of Persia by Arab traders on a yearly basis. Moses was commanded to take myrrh with him from Egypt so that the children of Israel could continue their worship. The Hebrews would mix it in their wine and drink it to awaken their spirit before participating in religious rituals.

Scents and smells arouse the whole spectrum of moods

and emotions, not just those of the more elevated kind. Odours can make us happy, hungry, depressed, sad, angry, or horny, without our even being aware of the cause. Each of our moods has its own particular odour. Wild animals may attack a human being because they smell their fear. Wild roses are used in aromatherapy to relieve depression, as are marjoram and thyme, known to be happy, uplifting plants. Ylang-ylang soothes a fit of anger; camphor and cinnamon are said to promote vivid images in the mind. Musk has always been known to arouse sexual feelings, and actually generates a hormonal change in the woman who smells it.[9]

The marketing departments of commercial concerns are well ·aware of the influence of smell on the consumer. Advertisements have carried the actual odour of the leather trim of a Rolls Royce; estate agents have been known to spray happy-family-type cooking smells through an empty house; restaurants place their air duct outlets at pavement level and waft mouth-watering smells into the street. Ironically, we are becoming more desensitized to natural smells by the persistent efforts of manufacturers to persuade us that our own natural odour is offensive and needs to be covered up with their product. We are also dulling our noses by an increasing preoccupation with sanitation and cleanliness.

Air-conditioned, sanitized homes are in danger of cutting us off from our root in the natural world. Because smell is so unconscious a sense, we might even imagine that we would barely miss it. Anosmia, however – the absence of the sense of smell – is a deeply distressing disability. Laura Croker poignantly described her suffering in an article on anosmia:

> A tint in our emotional spectrum is missing. I yearn to bury my face in hyacinths and enjoy memories of spring sunshine. I long to tiptoe into my children's bedrooms and inhale the warm sleeping smell in their hair, or to savour chocolate as a perfume, and not just as a soft sweet lump on my tongue . . . and to know when food is cooked before the smoke alarm tells me.[10]

Another sufferer, Judith Birnberg, had her sudden loss of smell reversed for a brief period by prednisone, an anti-inflammatory steroid which diminished the swelling that was found near her olfactory nerves. At breakfast the next day she caught her husband's scent and

> fell on him in tears of joy and started sniffing him, unable to stop . . . I had always thought I would sacrifice smell to taste if I had to choose between the two, but I suddenly realized how much I had missed . . . everything smells . . . now I inhaled all odours, good and bad, as if drunk.[11]

Mrs Birnberg had to reduce her intake of prednisone for safety's sake, and her sense of smell disappeared again. With it went a degree of emotional nourishment that the rest of us often enjoy without even realizing it.

ℰVOCATIONS

Smells creep into our memory as no other sense impressions are able to do, winding themselves around the events of our lives so tightly that our individual history is registered in a code of smells that only we have the key to. So deep into the anterior of our brains do the impressions of smell enter that our frontal, conscious lobes cannot always, or even often, recall at will the aromas that have lodged there and the events they are evocative of. The smell of a situation is not what usually springs to mind. People's words, or the shapes and colours in a room, the texture of a tabletop, are all more available to conscious recall. The smell of an event is a direct transmission of the nature of the overall experience, rather than an awareness of its distinct and separate parts. The instinctual nature of smell, its ability to inform us of the crux of a situation rather than its more obvious features, lingers on in our language with such phrases as 'to smell a rat', 'to smell an opportunity', and 'to smell something fishy'.

The chance encounter with a smell, then, will often unlock a forgotten moment. Charles Dickens claimed that the merest hint of the type of paste used to fasten labels to bottles would plunge him into the anguish of his early years, when bankruptcy had forced his father to abandon him in a warehouse where they made such bottles.[12] I had my own experience of the power of a scent over memory recently in

Branscombe, one of those Devon villages that fit perfectly on to a picture postcard. I was walking past a cottage of toytown proportions whose front was strung with roses and whose door was arched in honeysuckle. Ordinarily, I would have leant towards the roses, but this particular morning something more humble caught my attention. As I walked past the door, a faint tang somewhat like pepper, not entirely pleasant but not unpleasant either, turned my head.

A pot of geraniums was hanging from the porch, and as my nose caught their smell I was shot back to the time when I was eight. On my way to school, I would pick a leaf from the geraniums that hung over our neighbour's garden wall and enjoy the tingling sensation it sparked off in my mouth. In that smell was the thrill of a private enjoyment, the pleasure of being out in the world on my own, in that exciting stretch of public domain that lay between the familiarity of home and the ordered safety of school.

Our entire past lies buried somewhere in olfactory memory. That old armchair, the one in which your father used to tell you stories – its odour insinuated its way into your skin and became part of your personal flavour; so did the other smells of your mother's house; your father's car; the family pet; and the smell of the changing rooms in the school gym; the leather of your satchel, and shoe polish; the fragrance in the hair of the first person you kissed, the smell of their clothes and the smell of the dark in the local cinema; and even the smell of blood seeping out of a graze on your knee; dog shit on your shoe, and the smell of the corner sweet-shop. The whiff of early successes and failures still lingers even now, along with all the smells of rain: dank smells under bridges; the soggy wet of clothes on your back in a sudden shower; the fresh scent of rain falling in beech-woods; long meadows and busy streets and buildings glistening with the soot of an earlier century. And somewhere in all of us hides the smell of old age, the soothing smell of old woollies and soft-boiled egg with brown-bread fingers all over again.

There are other times when smell is close to the surface of a situation, and within easy reach of conscious recall. The sweat lodge I took part in at Lone Pine, California, left its impression on me through smell more than anything else. Every time I smell sage I remember the dark and clammy intimacy of that place. A sweat lodge is a ritual of the North American Indians which has been adopted by White people in America and Europe. Once a religious rite, it is now more of a purification ritual in which people shed their masks and sweat out whatever kernel of truth they are able to find in themselves. Volcanic rocks are heated on a wood fire and placed in a pit in the centre of a dome of plaited branches, often willow, which is covered with tarpaulin and blankets or, ideally, clods of earth. With everyone in, the leader of the lodge closes the door and plunges the participants into the womb of darkness. Then he pours water on the stones, and sprinkles sage on them. This serves as a sauna and sends waves of heat rolling around the darkness. Everyone in the lodge has four opportunities to speak – to dedicate an offering, to make a confession, to say a prayer, or to speak whatever is on their mind. At the end of a round of speaking, the leader pours more water on the stones. By the end of the four rounds of this particular sweat, I had been reduced to a wet rag, and it was all I could do to crawl out of the darkness at the end and collapse into the cool of the water hole outside. Yet no amount of water will ever wash away the memory of that pungent darkness. The mingled sweat of twenty bodies, male and female, sweetened with the damp smell of the grass and the earth beneath us; the sage on the fire, the clammy mustiness of the dark air, the clean, dry kick at the back of the nose whenever more water was poured on the stones; the smell of wet wood and sodden blankets; all of these in one tangled cloud that gathered us into an intimacy evocative of some primeval womb. That morning our borders were melted down and our combined essence sent out into the crispness of dawn a signal that all humans, whatever their differences, are reducible to a few common elements that even the dullest nose could smell on the wind.

The Fragrance of the Soul

Our individual odour is an alchemy of many constituents. Our particular mix will depend on the food we eat; the amount of hair on our body; whether we wash, and with which soap and shampoo; the mood we are in; our state of health; and our general disposition towards life. Though we may be oblivious to it ourselves, those close to us will recognize our distinctive aroma as soon as we enter a room. We leave a trace of ourselves wherever we go, as any dog will know; although the capacity of humans to recognize a smell varies from one individual to another by as much as 2000 to one.

Helen Keller, like some others, was capable of walking into a room and describing the mood of the people who had been in it last. She could distinguish the smells of fear, happiness, or anger. She describes eloquently the odour of men:

> *Masculine exhalations are as a rule stronger, more vivid, more widely differentiated than those of women. In the odour of young men there is something elemental, as of fire, storm, and salt sea. It pulsates with buoyancy and desire. It suggests all things strong and beautiful, and joyous, and gives me a sense of physical happiness.*[13]

This, from someone who was both deaf and blind. The hero

of Patrick Susskind's novel, *Perfume*, can smell the mood of a cow from a glass of its milk. In Inuit tribes, the common greeting of rubbing noses has its utilitarian basis in 'smelling out' the intentions of the other person. In Asian countries, such as Borneo, Burma, and India, the word for 'kiss' also means 'smell'.

Someone who eats meat every day and a large proportion of processed and fatty foods will have a very different odour to a vegetarian who eats fresh vegetables, grains, and fruit. The former will smell more pungent, sometimes even faintly rancid. The latter will smell fresher and sweeter. Perhaps some people with sensitive noses are vegetarians for this reason. Lady Dorothea Neville, during the siege of Paris in 1871 when some of the richer Parisians ate the zoo animals, wrote, 'I rather enjoyed the donkey, although it was a little dry, but I never partook of it further, it made me stink.'[14] Anyone from the Far East could smell Susskind's hero and know that he had drunk milk as soon as he entered the room. The Japanese rarely eat milk products after weaning, and find their odour in Westerners distasteful. The odour of the Japanese themselves is delicate to the point of being neutral, a reflection of their staple diet of soya, rice, and lightly steamed vegetables. This subtlety of scent is also due to Asiatics having fewer apocrine glands at the base of their hair follicles than Europeans do. At one time, a strong body odour could disqualify a man from Japanese military service.[15]

As health has its particular odour, so too does sickness. Several illnesses can be diagnosed by their distinctive smell. The fruity aroma of advanced diabetes is well known, as is the fishy, urinous breath of kidney failure. Diptheria is sweetish, typhoid fever smells like 'baked bread', and the odour of gout is described as resembling a petshop.[16] In the Tibetan system of medicine, among others, smell remains an integral part of diagnosis. A doctor has described the visit of Yeshe Donden, the Dalai Lama's physician at the time, to the ward of his local hospital in America. It had been agreed that Yeshe Donden would examine a patient selected by the hospital medical team.

> *The air in the room is heavy with ill-concealed dubiety and suspicion of bamboozlement . . . for the past two hours Yeshe Donden has purified himself by bathing, fasting, and prayer. I, having breakfasted well, performed only the most desultory of ablutions, and given no thought at all to my soul, glance furtively at my fellows. Suddenly, we seem a soiled, uncouth lot.*

The doctor describes how the Tibetan holds the patient's wrist and takes her various pulses while in a state of meditation. Then he pours a specimen of her urine into a bowl,

> *and proceeds to whip the liquid with two sticks. This he does for several minutes until a foam is raised. Then, bowing above the bowl, he inhales the odour three times. He sets down the bowl and turns to leave. All this while, he has not uttered a single word.*[17]

From his meditations on the woman's pulses and the odours of her urine, Yeshe Donden proceeded to give a minutely accurate diagnosis of her disease.

It is the tongue and nose together which discern the flavour of a person. Their flavour is the combination of the taste they leave in the mouth and the smell they leave in the air. Our individual flavour is our hallmark and, perhaps because the language of smell is so halting, we use the vocabulary of the taste buds to describe another's essence. We all know people who are sweet, sour, bitter, and people who are the salt of the earth. Yet these descriptions are an attempt to capture not so much a person's taste, as their flavour: the particular blend of savour and smell that makes each individual who they are.

As Helen Keller knew, a mood will always leave a trace in the air. A mood prolonged and adopted as a habitual cast of mind, will etch its way into the features, and even into a person's gait. A mood can develop into the predominant colour of a person's soul, and we will catch their flavour whether we or they wish it or not. A person can, for example, be eaten away by bitterness, slowly, over a period of years, as iron is eroded by rust. This, I believe, was the fate of Mrs Rawlings. Her thin, angular body used to perch behind the counter of the village sweet shop and a metallic tang would seem to hang around her in the air, something like lemon juice in a chipped tin mug – quite discordant with the sugary, sticky things in her rows of glass jars. Her shoulders were tight and hunched together, her eyes were sharp, and would swing round the shop in sidelong glances, with the occasional accompaniment of some acid comment. I was no more than ten, but even then I wondered who she thought had done her wrong. Or was life itself the culprit, for not having materialized the dreams of her youth? I did not know, though I later discovered that Mrs Rawlings, like so many people with a bitter edge, had been unable to forgive.

Bitterness, even so, has its proper place in the scheme of things. The bitter taste of disillusion can help restore to proportion a life that may have been too sugary and shapeless. Disillusion is a *chastening* experience, that wonderful old English word. To chasten, to draw away the excess, to return to proportion, to induce a sense of humility, humour, a return to the solidity of earth. It is when disillusion worms its way into the deeper reaches and stays there feeding on wrongs, imagined or real, that it exudes its bitter flavour from a person's presence.

Salty people usually live close to the earth and its natural rhythms. They are strong stuff. There is a man who makes walnut oil in Sarlat, in the Dordogne region of France, with an oil press which has been working without interruption or modification since the sixteenth century. He speaks only the local patois, French being a foreign language for him. He received the press as a wedding gift from his wife's father, who worked it like his father before him. He does what his forefathers always did. He passes the local stream through the vat and squeezes out the finest walnut oil in all of France. He has never stepped out of his village, and his work is his life. He knows what he is here for, and he does it with a simplicity barely conceivable in the modern world. He exudes the heavy flavour of his oil and fruit. He has grown straight out of the local soil, just like the walnut trees that give him his living.

Sourness, on the other hand, is often a richness curdled, left too long or picked before its time. Sour people may be out of step; they may have shot their arrow too far or too short, even though they were moving in the right direction. Whereas bitterness might lash out in anger, sour grapes tend to turn to sadness. They make our eyes water. They carry a disappointment, the sadness of promise unfulfilled, dreams unlived, hopes withered on the stem. We know what sourness is: friendships turn sour; business deals go off; relations between countries take a turn for the worse. Yet the hint of vinegar about such times can give us something to bite on. The testy nature of a sour old fruit can prove our mettle. Oblivious to all airs and graces, these people can challenge us to stand our ground and speak the truth in plain language. They carry the dour, wry quality of a wrinkled crab apple.

When we call someone sweet, it is often a double-edged compliment, as if sweetness were not all we were looking for. The mango, after all, is exquisite precisely because its sweetness is tinged with traces of sharpness. In calling someone sweet, we may be implying there isn't much to them, that they are an easy touch, without much will or shape of their own. This, though, is the sweetness of refined sugar, rather than the natural sweetness that can exude from a person's soul. The prevailing diet of the developed world leans heavily on refined sugars and starches that take the edge off the shape of the body and dissolve its natural tone. This kind of sweetness is sickly. Sweetness of soul gives a fragrance that perfumes the air. It is a quality that has more of a scent than a taste, being less earthbound, more evocative and imponderable. The sweetness of saints is well known. Dante describes the Virgin as a rose, and the apostles as twelve lilies 'whose fragrance led mankind down the good path'.[18] The description of someone as having 'the odour of sanctity' was at one time taken literally. St Teresa of Avila was said to have wafted the whole room in which she was laid out in death with such a sweetness that the windows had to be opened. (Certain more cynical historians, however, are convinced her fragrance was due to chronic diabetes.) St Cajetan was said by his biographer to have had the perfume of the orange blossom, while St Francis of Paul is known for smelling of musk.

I came too late in this world to know these old saints and the veracity of their perfume. Yet I am in time to know a saint in India who exudes a sweetness sweeter than the

finest hive. His name is Poonja.[19] His fragrance – how difficult it is to describe it, something that only the cliché of milk
and honey might approach – hangs in the air of his little
room and is breathed down in gulps by the stream of people
who come to see him. The presence of Poonja floats like a
feather on the warm Indian air. In his view, there is nothing
to teach. He simply lives in the delight of being and this is
his message which he emits like a flower, with plenty of
laughter. How he got this way, who can tell, except perhaps
for Rumi, that great Islamic poet and lover of God:

Light the incense!

You have to burn to be fragrant.

To scent the whole house

You have to burn to the ground.[20]

$\mathcal{L}$AND AND $\int$EA

This salty moisture on my breath – the same that whistles
through seashells – I can smell its intent on the keen edge of
this wind, coaxing me to spread myself upon these waves,
to let the sea air eat into my lungs and carry my inward parts
far and wide. Yet in the same moment, this is a bracing
breeze: my spine straightens, my tone returns, and my self
leaves a more tangible trace on the wind. It thrives on this
irony, the smell of sea air: it awakens vitality, it sharpens the
edge; yet it sings a lullaby of such longing as to dissolve the
most rugged individual back into his earliest beginnings.

Its damp, clinging moisture reaches back far beyond all the travails and sufferings of men. It is the result of the waves parting and the earth being born; it is the briny smell of the first life breathing, the first heaving of consciousness out of the sleeping deep. My own breath began there, in that primordial division, and my own breath returns to me now on this stiff ocean wind. The ceaseless turning and returning of all things is on the fresh cut of this brine that clings to my clothes now as I walk up this cliff away from Branscombe Mouth and the rainclouds into a fresher, brighter, light.

Not even the sea, though, can extinguish the perfume of the land. A merchant seaman once told me that he would always catch the smell of Australia some fifty miles from the coastline. The wind, blowing straight off the land, would fill his lungs with the scent of juniper. Then, as they continued on their voyage and approached the shores of Brazil, the heavy odour of rotting and flowering vegetation would turn him giddy, with its sudden contrast to several days just spent in the fresh clean wind of the South Atlantic.

A world away from the tropical odours of Brazil, the soft sweetness of rural southern England is a balm, especially at the end of a summer day. I was walking one June evening along the edge of a large field of stubble in Devon, just after the hay had been harvested. I had intended to follow the stream, but the slope of the field showered me with the wakening smell of its fresh-cut grass, and I turned and walked up the hill to sit in the middle of the yellow field. I was there for a few minutes, breathing the dry earth and essence of grass into my lungs, when the howl of a vixen cut through the air. On the far side of the field, some three or four hundred yards away, I could just make out the shape of the fox, with a young one by her side, loping along the edge of the wood. She stopped, and howled again. I sat stone still. There was only the smallest breath of wind. She ran into the undergrowth with her cub and reappeared a moment later on her own, staring in my direction. She howled again and ran a few yards closer. Over the next half-hour she crept slowly nearer, barking with every fresh approach, until she was no more than seventy yards away. Instead of making straight towards me, she followed an arc which placed her downwind. I remained still, but it wasn't my movements she was concerned with so much as my scent on the wind. That, I could do nothing about; I smelt human, and that spelt danger. We sat there in a stand-off for another ten minutes, her head cocked first this way then that, until she finally decided I was not worth the bother, and retreated, with several more barks along the way, to the wood.

The land that fills my nose with delight more than any other, though, is Provence. Its scents and smells are all of the vital, invigorating kind. The land itself has the smell of latent fire, ashes, dry dust, whitened bone. I can remember no lulling smell reaching my nose, no odour of fragrance that has ever made me heavy or drowsy with sleep. This is a wakening land, of bushes with spikes and thorns, and of trees twisted into tight corners, full of electricity. Walk over the Col de Murs or along the top of the Grand Lubéron, and the umbrella pines and tall conifers will fill the lungs with an alpine clarity. Even in the dulling heat of noon the face will tingle, as on an early morning in some colder, Scottish glen.

I am like a child in that hot and scented land. I cannot resist pulling at the shrubs and grasses that line the little roads I walk there. Rubbing the furry leaf of sage between my fingers, the plant releases its secret like a magic lamp; a thick wave shocks my nose and clears my head in an instant. I rub another leaf and wonder, since I am in an altered state already, sailing on this sudden injection of clarity and life, if sage is on the list of addictive drugs. Rosemary and thyme are sharper, lighter somehow; and they, too, carry me on my way with a lighter, freer step. One day, I was jogging up the hill to Joucas and as I turned the hill at the top I suddenly found myself, without warning, in the thick of the combined aroma of all these plants and more. They filled the air for several feet across the whole width of the road and revived my flagging legs. Then a little way down the hill on the other side a field of lavender gave me the verve not to falter and to keep running till I reached our door.

Nobody Farts in Dallas

Robert Doisneau, the photographer, said recently, 'You know the real change in the streets of Paris since I was young? They don't smell any more.'[21] I wonder if Doisneau believes that Paris is going the way of Dallas. Dallas is the quintessential modern city. I was there for a week this year, and I did not carry back a memory of a single smell. There is no one in the streets. No one walks, everyone rides. The shops are closeted in sanitized, air-conditioned malls. No one seems to work anywhere except in steel and glass fingers that point to the sky. I am sure they do, but they are just not to be seen. Nobody farts in Dallas. No dog dares to crap on the sidewalk. Street trading and street entertainment are against the law. The only people allowed to call out on street corners are preachers. It is against the law to play games in the street, to sleep in public or loiter on street corners. Even the roads are wide and long enough to dissipate the potential smell of exhaust fumes.

A city without smells is a city without soul. Dallas left me with the inescapable feeling of a city that was afraid of human beings.[22] The range of a city's smells indicates the variety and richness of its human life. City smells are the result of people up to their elbows in the toil of their trade; of ripe fruit and vegetables, fish markets and abattoirs; blacksmiths, mechanics, french polishers, furniture makers; the droppings of animals and sloppings out; bakers and street vendors; hot air from subway ventilators; the great stew of beggars' rags, rich peoples' perfume, and all the degrees in between them. The more people live the same uniform lives; the more they live by their heads and not by their hands; the more they live and work off the ground, twenty or fifty floors up in sealed-off, air-conditioned buildings, the fewer smells there will be. City smells are the result of hundreds of different physical activities, of throngs of people mingling on sidewalks, grasping the nettle and putting their backs into their lives.

It is true that is not all they are. Smells are the dark exhalations of Victorian industry which continue to cover people daily in soot in Rumanian cities. They are the putrid signals of vermin and disease, the foul stink of raw sewage that runs in the streets. They are the mountains of rotting garbage that collect every time the refuse collectors decide to strike.

Few people would want to live in the Paris or London of the last century. Even the London of forty years ago simmered in a lethal pea soup of a fog that lives on now only in the imagination of Americans brought up on the horror movies of the forties and fifties. Some smells are best behind us, so to speak; but perhaps we have carried our zeal for the scrubbing brush too far. 'Out, damned spot!' Not content with efficient sewage systems, Clean Air Acts, and regular waste disposal, we have closed down the cornershops in favour of refrigerated superstores, turned the inner-city markets into rows of boutiques and the Pompidou Centre, and exchanged the local bar and café for the piped music of deodorized brasseries. Smells chart the natural rhythms, the growth, the blossom, and the decay of all life. The more re-

moved our lives have become from those rhythms, the more
we fear life's scents and smells, and the more bottles we buy
of whatever promises to 'kill all known germs'. The Pompidou Centre has its place; so do the boutiques and Safeway
and Tesco. The advantages of modern living are clear. It may
not be so obvious what we have relinquished for the sake of
them.

Paris and London, even so, are unlikely to be neutered
to the status of a downtown Dallas. They are built of living
stone, for a start, more than of concrete, steel and glass.
Stone breathes. So does brick. Concrete just sits there, a
glum block. It is to stone what plastic is to wood. Steel and
glass feel strangely neutral. There is a life in the very structure of an elderly city that will not be easily exorcized by
even the most ardent purveyor of pine disinfectant in aero-
sol cans. There is the smell of former grandeur, around the
Opéra, at least, and the Louvre, and in Trafalgar Square.
There is the freshness of the great parks, Hyde Park and the
Bois de Boulogne; there is still the stench of urine in grimy
alleys, the smell of the trade of the remaining shoeshine
boys, and the distinctive odour of the city subways. The
London Underground, especially at Baker Street, has a
sweetish, rakish smell, somewhat like an overripe pear. The
Paris Métro is altogether stronger, more pungent, exciting
even; with more than a trace of black tobacco and stale alco-
hol, especially when one of the old trains pulls in.

The liveliest smells I know in London are all in the area

of Soho: the jumble of roasting coffee, sweet French pastries, Italian sauces, Greek *mezze*, Chinese roast duck and the heady lemon grass of Thai cooking. Berwick Street fruit and veg market adds its contribution of discarded cabbage leaves and yellowing grapes at the end of the day. Then Soho has a seedy air which adds to its flavour. There is the lingering smell of illicit sex, male pheromones floating in the air, the sweat and bustle of theatre audiences pouring on to the street, and the adrenalin of droves of people seeking some extra excitement.

In Paris, the Quartier Latin still sends an aroma of North African couscous and *merguez* across the Seine, along with the smell of books and hot caramelized nuts; while the area round the Pigalle manages to make Soho, by comparison, seem as if it had been freshly spring-cleaned. Then, there are still corner cafés in Paris which can hardly have changed since Doisneau photographed them in the forties and fifties. I know one in the Bastille quarter, the Café des Arts, with the same coat of paint it must have had two decades ago; a faded brown varnish on wooden panels erected in a more decorous age. The counter is wooden, as is the floor, and the natural material blends in with the overall flavour of white wine drunk by the old men in the morning, the sweet bite of aniseed, the remnants of Gauloise cigarettes and the ines-capable hint of garlic on the patron's breath. Together, these elements fuse into an odour which anyone would recognize as French.

There is soul in Paris yet, even though Doisneau must be correct in suggesting that the streets have been largely swept clean. It is true that for the full-blooded flavour of a city, northerners now have to go south and east, to lands which care little for hygiene regulations, and where life is still lived in the raw. Rome is already in a different olfactory league to Paris, and Naples is probably the most pungent city in Europe. The acrid odour of its alley cats is enough to penetrate the most blocked of noses.

The cities of Asia, however, present a whole symphony of smells. Even if his eyes are closed, the nose of the traveller to Benares will tell him that he has stepped into another world. Life is lived communally, in public more than in private, and it seethes and bubbles on the Benares streets. A thousand scents and smells vie for the attention at every turn: coriander, cumin, garam masala; incense of jasmin and sandalwood; warm yoghurt in huge tin tubs; garlands of roses and marigolds; buffalo hide; beggars' rags; sweet hair-oil; the sharp, bitter odour of burning bodies; the stench of a mangy dog, of dark water running in gutters, the droppings of a thousand cows; the sickly sweetness of ghee; the delicate invitation of fresh mango juice and pineapples, and the grime and sweat on the brows of tens of thousands of human bodies, all pressed together in the same narrow street.

It is all so much, all so insistent, that the whole adds up to a demand for surrender – let go and join in, let our city pour through your lungs and seep out of your pores so that the spirit of India can mix in your bones. You may not like all the smells of Benares, but like and dislike will never take you far beyond the confines of your own opinions. Suspending judgement on smells is not easy, because smell is so directly linked with emotion. Yet in being willing to open the lungs and let it all in, we are opening a door to a faculty in us that can see further than the end of our nose and the automatic emotions it arouses. Letting in such a tidal wave of odours and smells can awaken an ecstatic joy. In that ecstasy we may perceive that although Benares may not be clean, it has a heart that is beating strongly. Benares is alive – vitally, emotionally, and spiritually. It is the strong odour of that life that lifts on the evening wind there.

*R*OSES

One summer in the mid-seventies I taught English to foreign students of all nationalities at a residential summer school. The students along my corridor were all Libyans. Every corridor had a small lounge area, and each evening the Libyans would gather there and sing religious songs, sitting on the floor and swaying backwards and forwards to their rhythm. I loved their sense of community, their spontaneous gaiety, and their religious devotion. Most evenings I would join them for a while, and enter the singing whenever they sung the only refrain I could understand, 'La ilaha illa'llah!': 'There is no God but God!'

The first of these evenings was my initiation into rose-water. During the singing they would throw bottles of it all over each other, and over me. I had never smelled such a glorious fragrance. I felt inspired by it, uplifted and soothed all at the same time. It dotted my shirt, my hair, my face, my shoulders, and I drank in its sweet perfume with every breath. For some while after that summer school, I continued to buy rosewater and sprinkle it around my house, reliving the joy it had given me among the Libyans.

Ten years later, I took a journey through Turkey with my ten-year-old son. We had been travelling an hour or so on the bus from Ankara to Konya, and it was hot and dusty already by nine in the morning. The conductor got up and took something out of his bag. Then he came lurching down the bus, shaking the entire contents of a bottle of rosewater into the aisle and over the passengers. Again I was hit by an uplifting wave of delicate scent that revived my flagging spirits. The rosewater settled the dust and soothed my throat. I lay my head back and closed my eyes. There was something in that perfume which raised my thoughts beyond the present journey. Rosewater bathed my spirit, and I fell into a sense of union with life that I have not often known before or since. Everything was in its place; I was in place; and in that noisy bus bumping through Turkey, the world was singing.

The rose is rightfully the flower of love. I can see now the enraptured face of a gardener one morning in India. He tends the grounds of the tourist bungalow on the edge of Khajraho. He came to us one morning as we stepped out into the sunlight, holding a red rose before him. 'How beautiful!' he smiled in simple delight, 'How beautiful!' He put his prize under our noses and beamed as each of us breathed in the ecstasy of it. The joy on the gardener's face inspired me as much as the rose.

The rose holds a promise of perfection. Little else can look, feel, taste, and smell so divine. For many, it is the most finely wrought expression of beauty there can be. The floors of Cleopatra's palace were strewn knee-high in roses in honour of the visit of Mark Anthony. The Romans had a special festival, Rosalia, in honour of the flower. The thirteenth-century Sufi mystic, Yunus Emre, used to say that a rose sighed 'Allah, Allah' every time somebody smelled it.[23] Rosaries originally consisted of 165 dried, rolled-up rose petals, and the rose was the symbol of the Virgin Mary. The rose blooms in the open human heart and perfumes the one who has forgotten themselves and given their all to life. Rumi, whose tomb my son and I were on our way to visit in that bus to Konya, said this:

To die in life is to become life,
The wind stops skirting you
And Enters. All the roses, suddenly,
Are blooming in your skull.[24]

TOUCHING

Somehow I think we come into knowledge (unconscious)
of the most vital parts of the cosmos through touching
things.
D.H. Lawrence, letter to Blanche Jennings,
15 December 1908

Touch Memories

massaging hands along my back

a steel blade between thumb and forefinger

the corner of a building on a dark night

my dog's nose

a horse's flank

running water between my fingers

soft plasticine

a woman's thigh next to mine on a crowded bus

warm limestone in Provence

wind in my face

cuddling an infant

the coarse grain of an old church door

dandelion fluff

wet grass

sweat on my brow

a warm bird's egg

a round pebble

damp plaster on a cottage wall

a thick towel rubbing my shoulders

a wet sock on my foot

the sting of a nettle

a clammy hand

a brass doorknob

the furry skin of a ripe peach

fingers running through my hair

a dentist's injection freezing my mouth

COMING CLOSE

Touch draws us into life, and life into us. It places the world at the end of our fingers; it implies intimacy, connection, and a sense of merger. It is not surprising, then, that in a visual society touch, and kinaesthetic awareness in general, are *viewed* as dangerous. In cultures where the visual is less dominant – around the Mediterranean, in Arab countries, and in Africa, for instance – touching each other, especially someone of the same sex, is a natural part of daily communication. In a northern, Protestant culture which thrives on distance, on clear subject-object differentiation, merger is seen as a threat, a regression to childish dependency, and a loss of individuality. The main reason adults chatter on incessantly, whether or not anyone is listening, is so that visceral reality will not break through and embarrass them with a more directly physical and feeling exchange.

This does not mean that the body stops registering felt

impressions; just that they are not allowed into conscious-ness. So the split between body and mind deepens, remov-ing us from the ground of our being. For touch is the primary human experience. It is the first sense to develop, and the one out of which the other four grow, since they are all specialized outgrowths of tactile tissue. Our lives begin surrounded by the nurturing fluid of the womb, and the newborn infant's initial learning experiences come through contact. Babies can die if they are not held, and their cries are often for touch as much as for food. In *The Continuum Concept*[2] Jean Liedloff describes how the Yequana Indians of Brazil hold their babies constantly for the first two years. In many developing countries, it is common instinct for mothers to massage their babies, and Frédéric Leboyer has made a beautiful film of a mother in India massaging her baby. Tactile stimulation is a basic need, the lack of which is known as 'skin hunger'. Like undernourishment, touch deprivation leads to stunted growth, both physical and psychological. Massaged babies gain weight as much as fifty per cent faster than unmassaged babies.[3] Love, security, nurture, trust, affection, motion, all are conveyed through the maternal embrace – or not, as the case may be. The way we are handled in those early years will literally shape our future world, and determine how in touch we feel with it.

Touch is the most spontaneous and instinctive reaction of a child to the world about him. Children have their hands in everything. Through touching something, they can feel its life, and have an emotional response to it – be touched by it. Children squeeze mud between their fingers, play with sand, and pick up worms with an obvious delight that most adults have exchanged for a safer but more disconnected, and ultimately more dissatisfying, relationship with the world. And while adults are filling every available gap with words, children can sense the underlying atmosphere, and have an instinctive grasp of a social situation in a far more honest and immediate way than their parents.

We lose touch with ourselves when we do not trust our physical sensations. They can be too close to home and to truth for comfort. Somewhere, we still know that our intentions play constantly across each other's bodies, that we are always picking up each other's agendas, spoken or not; but to blow the gaffe on such information, to pay attention to it even, would be to threaten the status quo. It would take the lid off the conventions of visual society. It would cause breakdowns and break-ups and a huge sigh of relief. All over the white Protestant world, people would relax into their bodies at last. They would take their bodily life seriously instead of for granted. People would fall more easily into the centre of their lives again, knowing the centre is to be trusted; and they would laugh with a deeper laugh.

We all know this at heart; we all have at least an inkling of our need to touch and be touched. Even adults, after all, find it hard to keep their hands off 'safe' objects like the goods in a furniture store, or the bread in a baker's. Yet because of the taboos of our visual culture, in which distance needs to be preserved, our need for human touch, especially, has become marginalized into the twilight of the semi-conscious. We fail to sense the connections implicit in all the assortment of professional touches we pick up from doctors, nurses, osteopaths, masseurs, hairdressers, beauticians, manicurists, even dentists. We may not even notice the sub-liminal touch of the waiter, the cashier, or any number of people we make contact with in an ordinary day; yet they can alter our mood without our knowing it, and they will certainly determine our feelings towards the people concerned. In an experiment in two restaurants in Mississippi, waitresses brushed a number of diners on the hand or shoulder, as much as possible without their awareness of it. The customers who were touched consistently tipped the waitresses more. In a Boston experiment, a researcher left money in a phone booth and returned when she saw the next person pocket the money to ask if they had found what she lost. If the researcher touched them while asking for their help – insignificantly, so they didn't remember later – the likelihood of the money being returned rose from sixty-three per cent to ninety-six per cent.[4]

We like being touched, then, despite ourselves. Of course we do. It brings us to earth, to our own ground, and to the ground we share with others. It brings the life and the soul back into our world. And being the resourceful and dynamic culture it is, the West is beginning to cotton on.

Something in the cultural *Zeitgeist* knows now that our bodies are actually O.K. They are not inferior machines that we need constantly to drive to better results – to better race times, bigger biceps, or longer hours at the office. Neither are they an impediment to any spiritual salvation: on the contrary, they are the foundation for it, the very basis of a true religious sensibility. For the religious sensibility implies an openness of heart in which one may be moved, or touched, by life at the core of one's being. This is a literal, not only a metaphorical turn of phrase: the use of the words 'to be moved', or 'to be touched' in this way, reminds us that even the most subtle of feelings are physical sensations. This redemptive view of the body may not be common knowledge yet, but the news is certainly out. Sexuality is being acknowledged by an influential minority as a source of beauty, and not just as a means of self-gratification. Psychologists like Alexander Lowen and Stanley Kelemann have, for well over a decade, set new philosophical parameters which emphasize the centrality and wisdom of the body, while Frédéric Leboyer[5] has perhaps done more than anyone else to show the importance of touch to the newborn child. It is largely as a result of his efforts, and those of Michel Odent,[6] that waterbirthing, the placing of the newborn on the mother's stomach, and the delay in cutting the cord, form the basis of what is now known as natural childbirth.

Even so, many of us are stiff still, in the grip of an

'achieving' consciousness which is always straining for the future, and restrained by the conventions of a detached perspective on life. In its attitude to the body, and to body contact (as in every other sphere of life), the West is between worlds and moving fast in more directions than one. In a plural society, it is for each individual to determine his style; but a way of life that does not place trust and value in the body seems likely only to perpetuate the guilt and the contraction from physical existence that has characterized so much of the last few hundred years. The window is open for a change.

GREETINGS

Meetings and partings, beginnings and endings, all happen along the edge, where one world connects, collides, or departs from another. They are heightened moments, when we are more than usually aware of ourselves as well as of the other; and they bring an intensity of energy which is usually directed into bodily contact, or gesture. In earlier cultures, elaborate rituals were developed to allay or redirect the anxiety that could arise on such occasions. Much care would be given to acknowledging the honour of a person; gifts would be exchanged, and dance and music would play an integral part in bringing host and guest together.

In these cultures, it was not the individual who was honoured, so much as the rank or social caste that he represented. This is still the case in contemporary Japan, where bowing remains a common practice. The old European habits of doffing the cap and kissing the hand were likewise signs of respect, not just for the individual, but more for their social station and their gender. In India, the greeting of *namaste*, with palms together before the heart in a prayer position, salutes the divinity in a person, the universal dimension all of us share in, rather than the particular individual.

In the contemporary West, the formalities of rank and social station have largely been swept aside, leaving individuals to greet other individuals in the style that best suits their own attitude to life and to the particular occasion in hand. There is only a split second to deduce the appropriate greeting, and sometimes one's judgement can go hilariously astray. When the Italian psychologist Assagioli met the Indian philosopher Lama Govinda, Assagioli put his palms together in customary Indian fashion while, in the same instant, Lama Govinda held out his hand for a Western handshake. The first few seconds of their meeting were spent roaring with laughter.

In a global society, national customs have travelled far from their original borders and people all over the West, if not over a large part of the world, have many different greetings they can choose from. Even if there is no formal contact at all, the free-floating energy of the situation will channel itself through a touch on the shoulder, or a brush of the hand; or a passing of the fingers through one's own hair, a joining of one's own hands, a rubbing of the nose – all to confirm one's presence, touch base.

One customary greeting that has spread all over the developed world is the kiss on the cheek, traditionally associated with Europe. Today, this is usually used to greet a person of the opposite sex, or between women, though it probably harkens back to our remote ancestors who, taking their cue from the animals, would smell out any newcomer to get the lie of them. There can be genuine intimacy in an exchange at such close quarters: a mingling of odours; the feel of the cheek, that soft, sensitive area, contact with which can lead behind a person's social face. This, though, is more of an Anglo-Saxon version, without the formality of what in traditional kissing countries such as France is little more than a peck; a quick peck on both cheeks, which always leaves me with a feeling of no contact, or at most, a shiny clack of two surfaces whose fleeting proximity only highlights their distance.

Even the English can seem more honest, at least, than this, in their foot-shuffling lack of touch altogether; just a hello, and a glance of the eyes. The pain of it, though: like so many lemons, standing there in their fidgety aloneness, in the midst of a crowd of introductions.

The handshake, however, has a lot to say for itself, and is being adopted even in England, where until recently it was reserved for special occasions. The cynic might say that a handshake only serves to keep a person at arm's length, which would suit the Englishman perfectly. Yet there is a lot more to a handshake than that. You can feel the tempo, the temperature, of the other, and reveal your own to them. If the hand isn't too stiff, in a posture of fending off, you can feel the life in it, the pulse, the relative strength or weakness of character. You can feel their willingness, or the lack of it, to meet and be there with you. And with a handshake, you can look into a person's eyes.

That is not the case with a hug. You can make faces behind a person's back with a hug, or even stab them. This is the paradox of it: the closest contact of all can be the most deceitful. In the former Soviet Union and its satellite countries, the embrace of politicians in public was always regarded with cynicism. In the 1989 revolution, the Fidesz (Democratic) Party of Hungary ran a poster campaign showing the Hungarian Communist Party leader embracing the President of the U.S.S.R. Below them, a man and a woman were hugging amorously on a park bench. At the bottom of the poster ran the caption, 'Now You Can Choose'.

Not everywhere, then, does the hug meet with the same unmitigated approbation as it does among certain sections of the American population, notably on the West Coast, and in similar 'alternative' cultures in northern Europe. The Russians have had a much longer experience of the hug, so it is hardly surprising that they are more sensitive to its various shades of meaning. They would probably be quick

to detect the gushiness, rather than intimacy, that can sometimes be the hallmark of the Western hugger. There is even a
movement among new age men in America and Europe to
join the 'hugging warriors' – men who want to make a decla-
ration of their openness, their warmth and vulnerability to
each other in a full-bodied hug. The hug thereby becomes a
political act. Unfortunately, prescriptive behaviour tends to
defeat its own purpose. Like any spontaneous activity, the
hug becomes a charade when it is turned into a statement;
yet another way to avoid intimacy while feigning the
embrace of it. A spontaneous hug, on the other hand, is a
marvellous thing. Full-bodied contact with another person
can return one to oneself and to the fact of one's existence in
a relational world. It can affirm an openness to friendship,
warmth, and human exchange. It lays bare the physical
chest and the psychic heart. It confirms the old adage that in
defencelessness lies the greatest strength.

ANDS

Hands have a life of their own. They have a way of taking
hold of things before our social conditioning has time to stop
them. They are known to pick one more chocolate biscuit
from the box that we would have quite dared to; they finger
the bread in the baker's and the fruit in the grocer's; they
sometimes move instinctively to brush against another, to
hold their arm or spread over their back without stopping

first to consider the appropriateness of their action. I suppose I am talking about my own hands. My hands like to make contact; they enjoy the firm shake of another's hand, the grasp of a doorknob, the soft rasp of wool, the clutch of a squeegee ball. They like to have a hold on the world, a firm grip on the day, perhaps because both the day and the world slip easily sometimes through their fingers.

My hands enjoy the press and the rub of life, its slippery sheen, its give and take, its veins and creases, its knots and knobs and moisture. They draw pleasure from structure and form, from the curve and line of things, from angularities and corners, from the backs of chairs, from globes of the world, old fluted lamp-posts, stone sculptures of forgotten Buddhas in the back of a London museum, and plump strands of seaweed, there for the popping. I know the thrill of passing my hand round a Henry Moore sculpture and feeling the intelligence that poured from his hands into the stone, a tangible transmission beneath my fingers. It is a pleasure, too, to watch other people's hands: the flying fingers of a hairdresser; the dancing fingers of a pianist; a child tying his shoelaces; a woman doing up buttons at the back of her dress; a chef throwing his ingredients with a flourish into the pot; a trained artist deftly arranging flowers; a lover stroking her beloved's hair; the firm grip of the bat in a baseball game; someone knitting on the train.

I enjoy holding another person's hand, especially when my eyes are closed. It's a solid palm I am holding now, though not too solid, like a good spring mattress, broad, though not so broad as it is long. It's a dry hand, this one, with a map on the palm etched deep enough for my fingers to follow, two lines scored across the top from side to side, and another, with tributaries, heading north to south. Bones, fine like a bird's, fan their way across its back to the long straight fingers. Beneath the musculature I sense an intelligent stream running, telling me this is a hand which knows how to pluck ideas out of the air. I sense something else, as well, passing from this hand to mine, a human warmth, a compassion even, that knows how to stroke, to soothe and rub better; I imagine this hand would know to hold someone when all words were useless.

I am holding an entire life in my hand, its mystery, its darting lightness, its gravity, the throb of its engine. And I know now that they are holding my life in theirs. In the palm of their hand they have my hopes and fears, my dreams unfulfilled; letters half written and never posted; the old bee-sting that wouldn't die down; the tender grip of loves and friends; poems and essays that rolled off the pen; the sweat of searching for lines that wouldn't come; the blossoming of my lover's breast; the shy reaching out for a hand that wasn't there; the buttons of shirts, once so loved but now forgotten; and warm blood straight from the heart. There is more still: threepenny bits and old half-crowns; dry sand running through the fingers; sodden marigolds clinging to them in holy river water; the moist spring grass in a

Devon meadow; and a thousand shakings and wavings, farewells and welcomes.

EET

My feet are usually enclosed in layers of materials – wool, leather and man-made fibre – that insulate them from the touch of the world. It can't be helped. I live in the chilly north. It is all the more pleasurable for me, then, to run barefoot in the grass and feel the earth directly beneath my feet. Moist earth and morning grass, fresh with dew, on the soles of pale northern feet: I can feel it now. There is little to better it except perhaps the touch of warm rock – especially white rock, calcite, firm and hard – something solid to stand on that will carry my weight like a feather; or the give of wet sand along the shore, the sucking motion under the toes as the next wave rolls in. Feet are sensitive creatures, however thick-skinned they are. They know what they like and don't like; and though they warm in a general way to the touch of nature, they recoil from what might get us in trouble. They spring away from sticky surfaces and spiky things, and they are wary of worms and sea anemones and beetles, of tarmac and slippery bathrooms.

It is because they are sensitive to our wellbeing that they are a sure and steady guide to the explorable world. Feet are for standing on, for moving forwards into the world, for feeling our weight with, for taking up space and confirming we are here, with a rightful place. Standing up straight is a physical statement which says to the world, 'Here I am'. What a pleasure it is to feel the weight of one's body spread the balls of the feet on an old varnished floor.

Walking says, 'I am on my way, this is the way'. These are feet affirmations. The feet are our ground, our direct and constant contact with the reality of the daily world, and they express our intentions concerning it. Feet have their own earthy wisdom. Ask a blind person. Frankie Armstrong says she depends on her feet more than on her hands. Her feet, not her hands, know when to step down or up, or when to stop at the edge of a cliff. It is uncanny how blind people can sense changes in surfaces they have never trodden before. I walked recently with a blind friend, a sculptor, through a room he had never been in before, and he walked down the steps at the end before I had reached them, not faltering even at the first step.

It is the most intimate exchange, to have someone wash your feet. It is not only a sensual matter, soft wet hands slipping through soapy warm water between the toes and over the arches; it is an act laden with significance, a washing away of the dust, the cares of the world; the honouring of one person by another, an exchange of human presences. In some invisible way, the person being washed gives as much as he receives; in offering his feet into the hands of the other, he is offering his own foundations, the staff of his life, into safekeeping. It is an act of trust.

The sensitivity of feet is not limited to a capacity to distinguish safe from dangerous surfaces. In my year at university there was a student with no arms, called Frank. Frank would sit in lectures with his feet up on the desk and write all his notes with a pen between his toes. His writing was as fast and as accurate as anyone else's. Not content with that, he was also a fine painter, using the paintbrush in the same way as the pen. Feet are sensitive in another way. On their soles, they carry a map of the body, with every organ and limb having a point of connection there, and healing therapies like reflexology and shiatsu work on the whole body through the soles of the feet. If you want to know your partner's intimate details, take their foot and hold it with a delicate attention.

MOUTH

Lips, tongue, teeth, juices, the fruits of the face, androgyny of the mouth. Lips with the redness of life and warmth, a vivid cry of life to life, a celebration, a seduction, a laughing pout, an invitation to the merging of mouths, a beckoning to the dark wet antechamber which looms behind the protective portcullis of the glistening teeth. Lips massage and suck in the darting tongues, encourage them to dance tip to tip, to rear on their end, and to entwine themselves in the double snake of the Hermes staff. Tongues are for emerging, barely perceptible, wetting the lips and inviting the other to come inside; they are for licking with, for fanning the flames of the other's desire. Tongues are the conveyors of the natural juices, essences that we exchange in the heat of the moment. In passion, we drink deep from each other's well.

Our first kissing is of our mother's breast, and from the very start feeding, aggression, comfort, and sexuality are all intermingled as the intimate pleasure of the mouth. Perhaps it starts then, the pleasure of biting and being bitten. With the mouth we mingle past and present, not only the past of our own infancy but the remote origins of our race. Animals lick and sniff each other on first meeting, and apes and chimps have been observed kissing and embracing when wanting to make peace.

The meeting of lips can have many layers of meaning and intention. It can be an exploration of one's own and another's sensuality; it can be an expression of desire, of friendship, of loyalty to a superior, of spiritual blessing; or it can be an uncomplicated and innocent greeting. What shifts the emphasis from one shade of meaning to the next is partly a cultural phenomenon (there are Finnish tribes who bathe together in the nude but consider kissing indecent)[7] partly the context, and above all one's intentions. What is remarkable is that the lips can distinguish so quickly which level they are being approached on, and can respond appropriately in a split second. Imagine what it would be like if your hostess moved to greet you at the door of her dinner party and you slipped your tongue through her lips. The portcullis would probably bite it off - unless, that is, it was the very thing she had always wanted to happen. Touching always implies the opening of borders, the letting down of the drawbridge, and never so demonstrably as when lips kiss. The degree to which the borders are open is a matter not only of context, but also of unconscious and instantaneous negotiation.

Sometimes we get a different response than the one we bargained for. Christ knew all along, we are told, of the malevolent intentions of Judas. A kiss of deceit that purports to be endearing or friendly but is in effect a lie, is actually not difficult to detect. There is a coolness in the face, as well as in the lips, that one's own lips, if they are awake enough, can sense the cause of. It is difficult for the body to lie, and when you are kissing you don't usually speak. A person's soul is in a kiss; so in a kiss we reveal ourselves, and our spirits mingle.

They can mingle even in the faint brush of lip to lip, for everything lies in what is brought to the act – in the degree of presence, intelligence, and feeling – rather than any passionate display of intimacy. A kiss can open the door to a person's mystery, it can be a self-revelation, and it can strike a fire alight in a hidden heart. Many years ago, I remember, there was a woman I loved who I barely saw. When our lips eventually met, all the feeling, all the energy stored in our minds around the image of the other that we had harboured for so long, all of it came flooding into that first tentative touch of our lips. It was an age before our mouths even opened to let each other in. There was no need. We were already pouring into each other in silence.

It is not only lips that we kiss. We use our lips to touch people's hands and feet in a sign of respect, to kiss the earth of our native land after a long or dangerous journey, to feel the velvet of a rose, the bark of a tree, and in Salman Rushdie's case to kiss bread and books out of respect for their nourishment.[8] Chloe and I once went to the Immaculate Heart Monastery in California to meet Fr David Steindl-Rast.[9] As we were waiting in the little entrance hall, he came out of a side door and immediately took Chloe's hand and bowing, with his eyes on hers, he kissed the hand he held and welcomed her to the monastery. Both of us were struck by his gesture. It was so clear, so full of genuine honour and respect, and yet warm, with a fullness of feeling. It was a kiss that showed how sensuous a monk's life could be. How much there can be in so little.

One of the sensations I shall never forget is when I was licked by a Jersey cow. That slab of a tongue, hot with a steamy, grassy breath, rasping across the back of my hand on a gate to a field on the edge of Bath. That slow, grating rub, like a worn kitchen scourer, heaving itself lazily over my flesh with an undeniable empathy of beast to man. Less sloppy than a dog, slower of pace, more casual altogether than any animal I can think of, that Jersey cow had the time of day for me, or for anyone else who cared to lean over the gate and offer their salt. For it was that she was after, and for that we were worth it.

THE EMBRACE OF LOVE

How mysterious, that people can feel so intimate, so mingled of essence, without recourse to a single word. Intimate silence is restful and nourishing; it lies beneath the threshold of words, beneath the play of the mind altogether, in an osmotic domain of ebb and flow. In its presence, when we do speak, the words fall less from our mouths than from out of the reservoir of silence itself. Once spoken, the words leave no trace and, requiring no response, dissolve back into the space from which they came. It is effortless, talk like this, and it matters little what is said.

In such an atmosphere, anything or nothing may happen, and it doesn't matter which way events unfold. Just one of the ways it can go is towards the embrace of love. Without effort, without any forethought or anticipation, his hand may move lightly over her leg, feeling the fine contours of her graceful body, until eventually they lie together in a naked embrace before the fire, passing the heat of their union between each other, two kittens rolling in and out of each other's limbs without knowing which arm or leg belongs to who; their moisture mingling, their tongues savouring each other's skins, their hands slipping through each other's hair, stroking thighs, squeezing palms, caressing buttocks, neck, shoulders, everywhere; caressing and fondling in a leisurely dance that is complete in itself, with no other end in view but its present delight.

When we finally enter each other in the cocoon of this intimacy, the flames leap with a sudden vigour, the kittens become tigers, fierce eyes of animal ecstasy shine, our panting and crying resounds in the surrounding silence; until, our vigour spent, we return again to the slowness of white embers, neither of us moving more than our breathing demands. The slower the movement, the deeper an inner fire seems to glow, nuclear. It can draw even the stars down into our loving.

Falling over waterfalls and rapids together, flying through air, plunging in dark earth, we may finally emerge from this fusion of body and soul not only as one, but as three. When we come together in intimate silence something may be forged in our union, a clear crystal in both the man and the woman, that defines our individual edges with an uncommon light. This can be our most precious gift to each other. In some way we may never intend, our merging can return us to ourselves and make us more our own person than we ever were before.

 THE LIVING SCULPTURE

I have often wondered to what degree I was given a body, and to what degree I have made it up as I have gone along.

Of course, my family genes turned me out this way and not like the boy next door, whose parents were half the size of mine: their progeny seemed to stem from another race altogether, of Mediterranean stock, a far cry from my long and angular frame of strictly northern ration. Not just my family, then, but my race; and not just that, but the particular era, the place, and doubtless other influences as well, beyond my ken: the radiation in the air during my infancy, the smoke from my father's pipe – all of this and more besides went into the shaping of the particular form that would stand up in class when the teacher barked out the name Housden.

That time and place leave their indelible mark on our physical form was obvious when the Berlin Wall was opened and East surged forward to meet West again. All those faces that suddenly filled the papers and the television screens: they belonged to another era, one that faded away in the West with the Second World War. Their formality and sobriety, their propriety, even, was not only in the cast of their eyes and the frown on their brows; it was in the structure of their bones. It was in the way they stood, the way they held themselves; it was in the energy that emanated from their bodies. I had the same sensation as I have had looking at photographs of the forties. In a culture of free-for-all change, like the West, every decade seems to have its distinctive look which is not just a question of fashion, but a whole attitude, a style of approaching life, that etches itself into the face and the stance of the body.

In this sense, Housden, too, was unquestionably shaped by his time and place. Yet, though the foundations were long ago laid down, that shaping is a process that continues still today. For there is another influence that moulds my form as much as any of these givens of my inherited condition. That influence is myself. That is to say, the way I live and respond to life, the thoughts I have, the feelings I harbour, the values I stand by, the deceits I hide behind. All these things – some of which I know, many of which I don't – shape themselves into my bodily form. I would even say that they sculpt my form along their own lines; that my body, its bearing, its impression on the world, or lack of it, is the living embodiment of who I am.

My soul, then, lives through and as my body and its senses. It is the same with us all. Our gestures betray a mood, an attitude that has been shaping the curve of our arm, the arch of our back, for decades, usually without our suspecting it. The way we hold our head, open our mouth, wipe our face, purse our lips, grate our teeth, touch our nose, sit in a chair: the sign of our life is in all of them. I have noticed that, in my case, I touch my nose as much if not more than any other part of my body: I squeeze it, scratch its end, and tap its bridge; and in every one of these tiny nasal connections I am pouring myself in physical code out into the light of day. When I talk, my hands and arms dart about and slice the air like an Italian's; when I am sitting by myself in front of the window, someone in me dances the tips of my fingers on my thumb or waggles them like wands in the air. I don't know why. It is my body speaking its mind, secreting the moods and dreamings of the dwarves, the gargoyles, the wizards and the sages, the little-boy-lost and all the other beings who wander through my blood stream looking for an opportunity to reach the surface of my skin and dance a little in the light of the day. And if they can't shape a movement then they will run a warm flush or a sudden chill in the back, or they will pop up in an itch in the groin. To be in touch with their goings-on is to be in touch with my more inarticulate whispers.

The body, then, is a living, moving sculpture; one that can move with the times, that can change shape and colour according to the inner as well as the outer climate. When the inner and the outer are in harmony, the body has a quality of 'tone'. The Chinese call this tone *chi*, the Indians call it *prana*; Western esoteric traditions have called it the life-force. There is another word for it. Watch a person in Africa walking up from the river with a pot on their head and a cow by their side. They have it. It's called grace. When this energy is circulating freely, we feel like an instrument that has been properly tuned; relaxed, alive, streaming even; more receptive and permeable to ideas and sensibilities of feeling that a tenser or a slacker body would be opaque to.

When this tone is deliberately cultivated, it can develop

into a tangible presence. You can feel this presence in someone as soon as they enter a room. They have something substantial about them and, at the same time, a levity, a wakefulness of spirit that immediately lightens the air. They are at home in themselves, whatever the situation.

This alive at-homeness is rare in a culture like ours which places such store by the image of a person. In a culture with high regard for presentation and packaging, the pressure is on to keep up a good face, and a large proportion of our energy is spent in putting on a good front, puffing our chest out, and taking life on the chin. To accomplish this we need to hold our energy in the upper part of the torso, which makes us top-heavy, with large areas over the rest of our body left numb and deadened as a result. A good presentation, then, does not imply presence. 'He was always charming, courteous, perfectly gracious, in that hushed, musical voice of his,' writes D.H. Lawrence in *The Princess*. 'But absent. When all came to all, he just wasn't there.'[10]

The kind of presence I am referring to is more than natural charisma: it is a quality that has to be worked for. Peter Brook says:

> *To me, what matters is that one actor can stand motionless on the stage and rivet our attention, while another does not interest us at all. What is the difference? Where, chemically, physically, psychically, does it lie? Star quality? Personality? No, that's too easy and it's not an*

answer. In this question we can find the starting point of our whole art. . . .

A real actor is an imitation of a real person. What do I mean by a real person? A real person is someone who has developed himself to the point where he can open himself completely – with his body, his intelligence, with his feelings, so that none of these channels are blocked.'[11]

Brooks's actors agree that the work on the body was the foundation of their preparation for Brook's stage presentation of the *Mahabharata*. 'This body training,' says Vittorio Mezzogiorno, 'was not something empty, the acquisition of a particular style or fixed gesture vocabulary: you had to infuse every gesture and movement with your own life and meaning, you must commit all you have.' 'Brook wants to awaken everything that is within us, every finger, every cell,' says Andrzej Seweryn.[12]

Theatre, like the other arts, is a traditional way of integrating the mind and the feelings with the body – of 'unblocking the channels'. Another way is through a spiritual discipline. The word 'spiritual' has come to acquire connotations of the 'other-worldly', and yet for the practitioner, as distinct from the believer, it has always meant a discipline that is based firmly in the reality of the body's erotic energy and wisdom. Eastern traditions actually see the universe itself as a series of material gradations. Everything is vibration, and essentially material, the body being the slowest moving element on the human scale. In this view, there can be no separation between the spiritual and the material.

A secular and more contemporary discipline is that of psychology. While spiritual disciplines are more 'spirit'-directed (the marriage of the earth and sky elements in us) psychology, the study of psyche, is more soul-directed. Its primary concern, for many people, is the marriage of earth and water (emotions), usually a valuable, if not necessary, prerequisite for following the more ancient traditions. In their different ways, both psychology and spiritual discipline seek to return the flow of life to the body, and thereby to draw the practitioner into the living experience of the present moment. It is only in and through the body, after all, that the present can be lived.

> The aim of psychoanalysis, still unfulfilled, and still only half-conscious, is to return our souls to our bodies, to return ourselves to ourselves, and thus to overcome the state of self-alienation.[13]

The great task, in contemporary language, is not to experience God, but to experience one's own living reality, with body, mind, and feelings open to the world and in touch with each other.

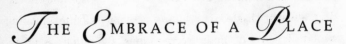

THE EMBRACE OF A PLACE

I had stood on this same ridge all those years ago, wanting to run down into the valley, as I had always done. Now, decades later, the memory was poignant still. That day, an unfamiliar feeling had passed over my chest and reined me in. Suddenly, I had felt too old for the valley. It was my twelfth birthday. Not being able to do what I had always done, not quite knowing what to do instead, I turned to amble home, a boat without a rudder, washed back by the tide.

I rested my hands on that same wooden gate, patched now with two stout branches tied with string, and drank in the fold of the meadow, and its remembered sweetness. My world had come full circle. Once again, the sweep of the valley, its steep incline, gathered me gently in its grip and held me close to a secret that no one else, it seemed, could catch the scent of. The triangle of creeper-filled wood over at one end, like a woman's hair between the fold of her thighs, drew me over the edge, as it had done so long ago; down through the unkempt grasses, along the stream, and through the kissing gate into another world. A musty world of dark, material things: brambles, burrs, stray branches of sturdy saplings, oozing mix of clay and rain. The valley trailed round my legs, pulled softly on my heels; and I felt my own sap rising as I tramped through the wildness.

I longed to reach those creepers again, those ones that had always dangled from the upper trees of the waiting wood. To fly on those creepers was a marvellous thing. Scrambling up the last few yards through lengthening shadows, I grabbed the first one I saw and hauled it as far up the wooded slope as I could manage. Then I gave it my full weight and sailed triumphantly over the undergrowth that had coaxed me all along to stay close to its earth.

From the moment I clutched it, the creeper assumed the proportions of an epic creature, a jungle python whose thick body filled my grip with the thrill of life; the coarse tail of a mammoth monkey whose fidelity, I suddenly realized, could not be taken for granted. It was then that the brittle creeper began to lose its own grip somewhere up in the higher reaches. From high in the treetops it delivered me in slow motion to the wandering tendrils of the thorns and the brambles. Yet even this fall had its own pleasure, its inevitability; and the primitive vigour of seeing my own blood mix with the mosses and in the damp earth.

The Feel of Southern Stone

Sitting on this rock that juts out from the dry earth like a giant's finger, my skin feels closer to the wind, and to the sea which is rolling in just beyond the far range of hills. The land itself passes through me too, imparting its familiar pulse to my receptive skin. I am never alone in Provence: a rough belonging warms my veins, the belonging of dogs who roll in the grass.

It is the work of gender, the complementary attraction of

opposite forces. My constitution has been soaked with the rain and the damp of southern England; it leans imperceptibly towards the dry and the heat of the south. But why not Andalucia, or Calabria? Or Tangiers, the coast of North Africa? It has something to do with proportion. The land in Provence holds rock in equal counterpoint to the green of cypress and purple of lavender; the dry earth has veins of river – the Nesque, the Verdon, the Var, and the great Rhone artery. Wild hills surround islands of civilized beauty: abbeys, villages and barns whose shape and material only heightens the free spirit of the land that hosts them; and towns: Avignon and Aix, fine testimonies to an older, more leisured European life. Other, more southern lands are harsher; their savage earth wages a war of attrition against any civilizing hand and cuts an indelible furrow of poverty into the lives of its people. There is in Provence a particular equipoise of domesticity and raw, elemental wildness that results in a beauty enhancing to both.

This beauty flowers in the rocks themselves, in the bluffs and crags that jut out among the stunted trees; in the white cliffs that stand out suddenly from the greener, tamer plain: the big and little Lubéron, the Mont Ventoux, the Mont Ste Victoire, the gaping quarry at Oppède. These are the rocks of ages, rocks of solid foundations. They hold the spirit of the land in trust. Even in their immobility they are alive with the faces of animals in their contours. They capture a trace of every living being that passes their way – perhaps to hold it up and startle future travellers from their dreams. The print of an entire people is in their dust.

There is a profound relief that comes from sitting on these stones. They are so thick with life, past and present, that they jolt me out of my narrow framework and join me immediately with everyone else who has passed this way. And there is more, for this angular crag is alive with a life of its own, quite distinct from the human life that has left its trace on it. For all its familiarity, the undeniable vitality of this rock is of a different order entirely than the life that pumps through my soft and fragile veins. There is something about its raw, uncut face that defies my attempt to tame it with a hand outstretched on its surface.

One day, I walked up the cliff at Lioux, wondering how it could stand there for so long without moving, a curtain of white rock drawn suddenly across a valley of vines. Being on the plateau at the top is like surfing on the crest of a giant wave, a great wall of water frozen in the moment it was about to break. From that high vantage point I could see other ,slabs of white in the distance, held equally in suspension over orchards, pathways, houses, and barns, all the fragile constructions of men. The French call these formidable tectonic creations of the earth's vitality by a name that says everything – *les massifs; les massifs de la haute Provence*.

Something of their massive personality remains even in the bits of them that are broken off and shaped into walls and pathways, chateaux and abbeys, barns and *mas*, the Provençal term for a farmhouse. The stone steps threading their way through Oppède or Joucas are like this. Every one has its own colour and texture. They have borne the weight of countless men, women, carts and donkeys for centuries and even now they take ungrudgingly the heavy plod of overweight tourists. Bowed in the middle from the ceaseless tread of feet, even so they seem impervious to time. They sit squarely next to each other as they have always done, held in place not by cement but by the original care of their makers; by the sharp southern light which chisels each edge, new every day, into stark and uncompromising relief; and by the friendly spread of lichen and coarse grasses.

Stone steps are everywhere here because there is always a hill to climb. Gordes, Joucas, Goult, Bonnieux, Roussillon, nearly every village is on some crest or rocky outcrop, and the houses rise easily, unobtrusively, from their natural foundations of spur and ridge. No architect ever held them in his mind; these buildings emerge from a centuries-old collaboration, a mutual understanding between nature and the local inhabitants. They knew, of course, to cut the stone thick to ensure cool summers and warmer winters; but they also knew, though not with a cerebral knowing, to allow each stone in a wall to make its own individual presence felt – to contribute its own irregularities and oddities to the larger whole.

The stone is not dressed, then; it stands there in a wall,

serving its function, with the rawness of its origins still upon it. There is not even the cosmetic and the security of cement to soften the load of stone upon stone. Instead of a uniform and orderly surface, any Provençal wall is a kaleidoscopic display of a thousand ways of catching the light, each stone pressing its edge against the sun in a different way to its neighbour. Houses, châteaux, and churches, they all stand sturdy and square, as if to emphasize the strong, glinting stuff of which they are made. Visitors and aged inhabitants alike reach out for the consoling touch of warmth this stone gives to any fleeting brush of the hand, and for the rough and reassuring softness of its weathered surface.

Yet the locals do not forget the sweat in these stones, nor that they are the brothers of those which still litter the vines and fields, stubborn as ever before the cut of the plough. No consolation, these: the bane, rather, of any good man who has tried his hand at taming the southern soil and extracting from it a living for his family. This thin and rocky land has never made it easy for a man to survive. A handful of olives and some garlic rubbed into rough bread: this, only a generation ago, was the staple fare for a shepherd or a man in the fields during the day. It is different now, with the villas of the rich strewn across the hillsides. The land remembers, though, and smiles to itself.

*I*N THE *H*OUSE OF *A*NIMA

She rolled slowly on her back and lay for a last few moments in the dark warmth of her bed. The rain, spattering intermittently against the window, made her cocoon feel all the more like a soft glove. She hugged the sheet and the eiderdown, an old flock one that her grandmother had made. These were the times when her dreams came floating to the surface, when her mind was wide open and the daily routine had not yet heaved into motion. This morning, it was different. No images had swum to the surface, and she was content to lie there with open eyes resting on the faded rose pattern of the eiderdown. For moments on end, she lay as in a waking trance, aware only that she was happy. The rain beat down, and she drew her long legs up to her stomach in a shudder of pleasure, smiling at the petulant morning outside.

Today, she would light the fire downstairs. Today, she would not step outside the door of her house, she would conduct no business, she would receive no callers. Today was to be her day, and she would spend it filling her house with herself; she would lay claim to her place.

Slipping at last from the cocoon of the covers, she sat on the bed with her feet on the carpet; a blue and red Turkish one with thick, coarse pile, woven by a dozen women outside a tent on the Anatolian plains: another world beneath the press of her feet. As she leaned her weight on the floor those women, their headbands dangling gold coins, silver bracelets all up their arms, flew up to meet her, sisters somehow, their fierce sense of belonging stretching across time. This morning, she knew she belonged; she belonged exactly where she was, in her tiny stone cottage in the Cotswolds, in England. She belonged there as unequivocally as those women had belonged to Anatolia.

She stood up at last, arching her back in a cat-like stretch, offering her breasts to the air of the day. Moving to the door, she fingered the brass handle in a morning ritual, as if it were the vestige of some Aladdin's lamp whose genie was somewhere still in the vicinity. The floor of the tiny landing creaked its daily welcome as her foot hit the hollow on her way to the bathroom. It hadn't always been a bathroom, of course. The villagers had told her that in living memory the local cobbler had lived in the cottage with his wife and six children. Two rooms upstairs and one down. Four of the children had slept where she now had her bath, an enamel Victorian one with claw feet and original brass taps. It stood without any apology in the middle of a room where tousled boys in short trousers had fought and argued and made up again, and had listened in giggles to the heaving love sounds of their parents across the landing. So many lives this little room had held, so many sorrows and hardships, so much warmth of human kinship had seeped into its walls since the first farm labourer had pushed open the front door almost 200 years ago. And now it was her bathroom, her personal relaxation room.

And yet . . . for all its inner transformations and changes of inhabitants, the house was the same as the one built by the estate hands who had brothers in the army at Waterloo. The same flat stones that they had placed on top of each other still held their place firmly today; more weathered, softened somewhat, their walls grew out of the hill still as if they had grown there by nature. It was a house with being, with a life of its own, like any organic thing; and it was that life that she had recognized and loved the moment she had walked through the crumbling front door. She had always felt the need of a home to belong to, and she had found it; or perhaps it had found her.

She lowered herself into the warm bath and lay up to her breasts in water made smooth with oil of lavender and pine. Trailing her arms along the sides of the bath, she stroked the roll top with the palm of her hands. How reassuring old enamel was, like stout china made for households inhabited by the likes of Christopher Robin, or Rupert Bear. Above her, the crossbeam of weathered oak spanned the room in an easy leap. It served now as her towel rail. This was the kind of house that was willing and able to adapt to the changing fortunes and styles of its inhabitants as a snake will happily slough off an old skin for a new one, and yet remain the same snake.

For an hour she lay there, between dream and waking,

turning the warm tap with her toe whenever the water cooled, letting her skin soften to marshmallow. Her whole world drifted lazily and at random across her bathtub until, at last, she remembered the fire waiting to be lit downstairs, and the coffee, Old Sumatran, that she had bought the day before.

She rubbed herself dry and ran down the crooked stairs, pushed open the stairway door, which was little more than five planks nailed together, and moved like a cat round the kitchen counter to put the coffeepot on the stove. Then she loped over to the fireplace and lit the fire she had laid the night before. It took hesitantly, filling the hearth with billowing smoke. You can almost stand up in that hearth. There are two heavy firedogs in it which on this day were straddled with logs almost two feet long. A hatch in the corner must have baked a thousand loaves for the cobbler's family; it was closed now, its retirement mutely stated by a thin film of spider's web that hung over its door. She stood her coffee precariously on the Van Gogh chair by the fire and fell into the sofa facing it. The sofa managed a muffled creak of disapproval, and they began to settle into the day together, the coffeepot, the sofa, the woman, the house and the fire.

The fire. Nothing had ever brought her back to life in her darkest hours more than the crackling heat of open flames. There had been times when the vitality of the fire had seemed to beat on her chest like the hands of a lifeguard. This fire spat into the chimney and blew more than a little smoke into the room. The logs had not lost their green yet, and the wind was fickle today, sweeping rain and then sunlight over the sky in rapid succession. Gradually, though, the flames took hold, the hearth was filled with an orange glow, and her body flushed in the warmth.

Her fire was for warming her marrow with, for infusing her spirit with the clean breath of light, for burning away the dross of her cares; it was for mellowing her day, for bringing her home, for setting her mind free to wander with dreams. The house was built round its hearth, a third skin for generations of inhabitants, and its heart, too, beat all the more strongly when its fire was lit. She knew this, and it was for the thick stone walls as well as for herself that she always struck the match. It was a ritual duty of winter that the house, not just the cold, demanded.

Hours passed. The dregs of the coffee were long cold in the pot; she had read and savoured Italo Calvino's story about a couple on a gastronomic adventure; she had ruminated over whether to go travelling again; she had sat for long spaces of time in silence, without any thought at all. It was into one of those silences that my knock on the door fell. She rose, and stood for an instant in front of the fire, its warmth striking her with a final transmission. She remembered her promise to herself, that she would see no one that day. Despite herself, seeing herself walk to the door as if she were another, she threw open the latch and let the light and the rain pour in.

ANIMAL CONNECTIONS

With the languid gestures of all India, the lean young man in the gingham dhoti passes his palm over the flank of his water buffalo, washing her clean with the dirty water of the immortal Ganges. Ganga always washes your dirt away, no matter how sullied she is herself. He is standing up to his thighs in the river, with his buffalo a little deeper in, up to the curve of her belly. She carries the baleful patience of her race in her eyes, and stands there in her element with only the occasional flap of an ear while her owner continues to pour buckets of holy water on her and rub her with white soap in wide, melodic sweeps of his hand. It is tangible, the affection that spreads out from that hand. This is no chore; it is a regular ritual, a prescribed meeting between man and beast at the end of the day.

The man works his way along the bony black body, pressing his fingers round the protruding haunches, down along the flank and the underbelly, till he reaches her head, its hard skull and its fleshy lips and nostrils trailing phlegm and water down into the river. He reaches his arm round her neck and gently swings her face round so that it gazes into his. Working the lather between her ears and down her forehead, he drenches her with a last pail of brown water and bends his brow to make contact with hers. Then, taking her curved horns in each hand and directing them to the bank, he slaps her on the flank and sends her ambling up the slope. He stands there for a moment, watching her go, with the wide-open slowness of the land he belongs to. Then, throwing a final bucket of the Ganges over his own head, he follows her with the lithe sway of a body that still has its natural rhythm.

An act of generosity reaches deeper than the skin and moves our inward parts. It can throw a subtle bridge between worlds that in ordinary circumstances would never meet. I once had a job in Oxford teaching Iranians English. One of my students had been a conscript in the Iranian Army and had been sent on a tour of duty in the remote northern mountains. It was winter. One morning he left his hut to go down to the river for some water. As he stood up from scooping his pail in the rushing water he found himself face to face with a large silver wolf. He was helpless. The wolf was hungry. The hard winter had made food scarce. If he made any move for his gun, the animal would pounce. The wolf gazed at him through slitted eyes, its hair quivering. The man began praying; praying to the wolf. Silently, he asked to be spared. His heart was racing, his whole body tingling, when suddenly the wolf turned and left. That evening, my friend heard a scratching at the door of the hut. It was the wolf. The man took half of his dinner, opened the window, and dropped it to the ground. The wolf ate the food and loped off back into the wilderness.

I once saw the birth of a long friendship between human and

animal take place before my own eyes. I was in a stable with a friend who was looking over a horse. She walked over and laid her right hand carefully on his head, stroking it gently with downward strokes to his twitching nostrils. She took in his fine legs and the high spirits that rustled in his tail and quivered perceptibly through his flanks. Slowly, she prised his lips apart with her two hands and bared his teeth. Then she led him by the halter into the paddock. Smoothing his flanks and haunches she felt his life tingling against her fingers. She raised his hooves in turn without him moving a muscle, and felt the power of vigour contained in stillness.

His owner saddled him for her, and her knees barely touched his body when he broke into a trot. Soon they were cantering strongly against a big, scudding sky. The power in his belly flowed freely through her thighs and around her body. Every rider knows the joy of those moments when they and their horse are moving as one entity, one gathered rhythm of life pounding over the flying clay.

The woman fell into that rhythm with Jeddah then, and has never left it since. That he could echo that organic pulse, and that they could pass it back and forth through each other in a simple touch was a wholly unexpected blessing to her. Many horses, like people, have had their primitive power dimmed, or even tamed out of them altogether. She bought him immediately for the asking price, and she has been thankful to life ever since for bringing her an animal whose original freedom was still in his veins.

THE HEALING TOUCH

Imagine being on the edge of life, one's physical resources at their lowest ebb, death creeping along the edges of the hotel room in Delhi, reducing all movement to the fragile flit of a shadow. Marion Woodman was such a shadow once, keeping to this world by the slenderest of threads – held here by her love for her dog, without which she would happily have exchanged her aching body for whatever might await a departing soul. In this condition, she was sitting on a couch one day in the hotel lounge, writing a letter.

A large Indian woman in gold-trimmed sari squeezed between me and the side of the couch. Her fat arm was soft and warm. I pulled away to make room to write. She cuddled against me. I moved again. She moved. I smiled. She smiled. She spoke no English. By the time I finished my letter, we were both at the other end of the couch, her body snuggling close to mine. Still fearful of going outside, I returned to the lounge the next day. The same dignified lady appeared; the same game went on. And so for several days. Then as I was leaving one morning, an Indian man stepped up.

'You're all right now,' he said.

'What do you mean?' I asked, startled at his intimacy.

'You were dying,' he said. 'You had the aloneness of the dying. I sent my wife to sit with you. I knew the warmth of her body would bring you back to life. She won't need to come again.'[14]

I was lying on a table under the sky in Big Sur. The Pacific rollers were breaking behind me, and out on the horizon the sun was falling to meet the sea. With long, deep strokes she worked her way up my legs, dissolving the accumulated tensions of travel, and stirring the life back to my muscles. Over my back her hands flowed, along my spine and out to my shoulders. For the first time that day I felt the breath moving in and out of my lungs. I could feel the attention in her fingers, listening to the pulse of my body as they moved, and I could feel her breath beginning to join the rhythm of mine. A wave of gratitude rolled out of me and followed her hands. Then a wave of sadness welled out of nowhere, and for a moment I shed tears from some deep and shaded well. A relief followed that softened my whole frame, enabling her work to enter deeper still. Not one muscle did she leave untouched. My back, my front, my head, my eyes and lips, ears and nose, my feet, my hands and arms, all were oiled and cleansed by her loving touch. I felt profoundly cared for and more precisely, I felt understood. This massage was the most intimate communion of human warmth I had known outside the sexual embrace. That hour on the table overlooking the sea was one of the most sensuous I have ever spent. In passing the sense of her soul through her fingers, she returned the living soul to me. When she had finished, she left me alone on the table and I lay there with the slap of the waves, and the quiet joy of life returned to my veins.

$\mathcal{L}$ISTENING

I am just as deaf as I am blind . . . . Deafness is a much worse misfortune. For it means the loss of the most vital stimulus – the sound of the voice that brings language, sets thoughts astir and keeps us in the intellectual company of man.

**Helen Keller in a letter to Dr J. Kerr-Love,
31 March 1910**[1]

Sound Memories

The whirr of my grandmother's sewing machine as her feet pressed the treadle

The lazy drone of a biplane in a clear sky over an empty valley

The hurried flapping of wings above my head in a dark wood

Sudden birdsong one spring morning

The wailing hoot of a freight train passing across America

The thwack of the headmaster's cane on my backside

The whirring of cicadas on a summer evening in Provence
The huff and puff of The Windsor Castle *steam train pulling out of Bathampton Station*

The roar of the crowd at a rugby match

The sucking and rustling of pebbles as the sea withdraws

The patter of rain on the old tin roof of my parents' toilet

The tock of a grandfather clock

Ca y est! The cry of a newspaper vendor in Toulouse, announcing the end of the world every morning

The barking wail of a fox in Bristol at nightfall

The spitting of angry words from a boy in my primary school

The crack of sudden thunder

Our dog, a little black mongrel, barking and snapping at the postman

Church bells in the village

$\mathcal{T}$UNING $\mathcal{I}$N

The ears are the first sense organ to awaken, for the foetus can hear in the dark of the womb; and hearing is the last sense to fade away at death. Human beings were made to be listening creatures, and our ancestors lived in an oral community, where listening was as primary as seeing. Our forefathers crouched in the hollows of the great plains and listened intently to all the noises of the surrounding world, all those wild and mysterious sounds rising in animal throats and floating on the wind from the forests and the rivers; to the swaying of the leaves and the grasses, the rustling of snakes and reptiles, the flapping of wings and the falling rain in an evening sky. In an oral community, sound could travel far, for the world was alive in a different way. Into this century, people in Jamaica would lean against a tree and listen for messages from friends who were speaking into another tree a hundred miles away. In Shakespeare's time, the lines of a play were spoken 'trippingly on the tongue'; an audience could easily understand a performance in which the actors spoke twice as fast as today.[2] In Europe, prior to the nineteenth century, the life of the community and the nation would still be shared in stories, songs and ballads, passed from one hearth and one town square to the other. Music was a collective activity, played in groups and listened to by live audiences. Only in the late eighteenth century did songs and ballads become widely available in print.

In 1819, everything changed. The high-speed printing press had arrived. The gradual shift from the listening ear to the reading eye was dramatically accelerated, and the interior world of the private individual began to take precedence over the collective values of the oral tradition. It was only in the eighteenth century that the novel was developed as a literary form. In English literature, for instance, Henry Fielding's *Tom Jones*, published in 1749, stands at the crossroads between prose fiction intended to be read aloud in company, and that intended to be read to oneself.[3] In the nineteenth century the novel, the literary embodiment of subjective reality, became readily available to the wider general public for their private enjoyment. Though books were still read aloud in the family setting – mostly in the form of father reading from the bible – the fate of the ear was already sealed. Since then, we have seen the progressive elimination of oral culture from the Western world, to the point where the individual can now listen to all the music he wants, from anywhere in the world, in the privacy of his own living room; where he can also receive images informing him of events around the globe without having to move beyond his front door. Even the telephone, now the main conveyor of the human, if disembodied voice, is beginning to be replaced by the fax.

The eye so dominates our contemporary world that we

barely any longer have ears that hear. For many of us, a dead silence has fallen upon the listening ear. The only sense of belonging that many people have is the feeling of watching the same television programme as millions of others, and of being affected by the same events that flash each night into everyone's living rooms. Even in a room full of people, the individual is watching the screen alone, and in silence. The separate members of a family sit alone together, their conversation sucked out of them by the flickering intruder in the corner. With less and less to say to each other, there is less and less to hear. We have created a remote-controlled world where alienation, loneliness and despair are among the culture's most prevalent and resistant problems. We have deprived ourselves of two of humankind's most ancient and fundamental pleasures, the pleasures of listening and telling.

For the ear is first and foremost the organ of interaction, of human exchange and interdependence. It is hardly surprising that its use has been eclipsed in a world which exalts the image and value of the self-sufficient individual. On the other hand, the shift from ear to eye, from community to individual, marks a truly evolutionary step for humankind. We are witnessing the progressive individualization of the person from out of the conforming culture of collective values. Through the stimulus of the alienation that the disappearance of oral culture has generated, increasing numbers of people are turning their ears inwards and listening to themselves. They are developing meaning and value through the subjective life of their own thoughts and feelings. In an oral community, the individual primarily constructs his identity from association with his tribe or nation: he is first and foremost an Inuit, a Mayan, or a Dogon. Then it is his surname, his particular family membership, that identifies him more specifically. An individual in the West strives to find his identity through his uniqueness: by making his own particular mark on the world, and/or by discovering his own unique story within the contents of his own soul. Since the Renaissance, this has been the guiding theme of Western art; in this century, and more particularly in the last twenty years, it has also been the business of therapy. Therapy has emerged to address the need of people both to be heard and to listen to themselves; to discover and act upon their own story.

The danger of the therapy room, however, which is also its gift, is that it can serve as a womb set apart from the voices of the world. It can perpetuate the divide that so many people feel between themselves and life at large. I heard the poet, Robert Bly, say recently, and only partly in jest, that analysts should have a cow in their room, to remind their clients of the instinctual wisdom of nature. At the turn of the twentieth century, it is our outer ears as well as our inner ones which need to wake up again. It is a matter of both/and, not either/or. The art of listening to our own inner world is essential. At the same time, the world of the myriad of forms has been speaking for more than a century now without being heard. If we lend an ear not only will the world spring alive again in its own right but also, I suspect, we shall hear more easily an echo of the deeper sounds in ourselves that we may have been straining so hard (and perhaps expensively) to catch the meaning of.

We are set in the world, after all, not above or below it. We are interdependent with all the creatures and things it comprises, from the stars to the bowels of the earth. And it is above all through the ear that the world of living beings can enter us and make our life fertile. It is no mere whim that makes the men of the Dogon tribe in Africa whisper in the ear of their women before joining with them to conceive a child. It is no crude medieval fantasy that depicts in painting and fresco the Annunciation as a stream of golden light pouring from the Angel Gabriel into the ear of the Virgin Mary. Sound impregnates; it brings forth light, creativity, relationship, our deepest longings and desires. It was with wise words that the serpent awoke the soul of Eve. We would do well to listen, and the most natural place to begin is where we are, with who we are.

Ancient India had and still has its mantras, secret sound formulas designed to awaken the original sound of ourselves and of Creation. The Tibetans have their esoteric incantations and overtones to generate different mental states. Though we may learn these techniques with benefit, they do not arise out of our own cultural dilemma, and cannot, I would say, finally respond to the particular conditions of our time. We must start where we are, with what we have: a wholly secular world that has forgotten the essential names of living things. Foreign syllables will not do; nor even, ultimately, will the memoribilia of our own past. Though our past, along with present living traditions, can inspire us along the way, we need to start afresh.

We do not know or, rather, we have forgotten, the sound of the world. Our own words and language muffle and swathe what the things and doings of the world are telling us. To listen again, we need to fall below the noise of our own talking and allow spaces for the rhythms and voices of our everyday life. For they have been speaking to us all along in a language we knew but never remembered.

*L*ISTENING TO AN *O*RDINARY *M*ORNING

I awaken to the tide of my own breath and the softer breathing of my love beside me. In the far distance a pneumatic drill whirs, a city cicada. My stomach gurgles, the bed-clothes rustle, and as my eyes fall closed again I hear the keening wind whipping at the corner of the building and the seagulls wailing. The church clock strikes eight and startles a memory to life. I used to lie half-awake in my bed as a boy and wait for a church clock to chime eight, the very last moment I could lie there before having to leap out and get dressed to run down to the village school. No school awaits me now, but a breathing woman by my side and a day which I must carve from my own block.

The very thought brings the thud of my feet on to the old wooden floor, the gushing of water into the bath, the lapping, the rush, the gurgle of the excess down the overflow as I climb in, the dripping of suds down my face, the muffled rub of towel on my back, the sudden sound of my own voice talking to itself, the bathplug popping out and the water sucking away with a protesting gurgle: so many sounds I'll explode if I let them all in . . .

The floorboards creak in the kitchen and the spring-loaded door of the cupboard snaps shut as the kettle hisses and the gas on the hob puffs and blows and a rose petal drops to the floor from a vase with a resounding silence. In the bathroom my son clears his throat of phlegm and instantly I am in India where a hundred million men all snort up their phlegm at the same time every morning: the sound is deafening. A throaty liquid snort overwhelms all other sounds and awakens my repulsion quicker than anything I know . . . But the world rights itself and rustling tea leaves emerge, the tinny grate of a milk top scratching the table, and an alarm clock ticking while boiling milk is seething on a breakfast seashore. I am disappearing into a sea of sound. The tapping of a boiled egg, the crackle of toast in the teeth, voices starting into motion, the tuneless singing of a nine-year-old girl, the caw of crows, the clink of teaspoon on cup, and the lapping of liquid on china: there is nothing but the Word spoken by every object in its own tongue, a vast orchestra of living beings, the world announcing itself in a constant daily chorus of whispers and rumbles and gurgles and plaintive cries and pips and squeaks and running water blowing and calling out for no other reason than the love of being alive.

CONVERSATIONS

A good conversation loosens us up, unclogs the ears, gets our juices moving and our eyes sparkling. It is a bodily thing, it engages all of the senses, which is why the telephone is so inadequate for it. You can feel the thread of the talking between your fingers, see the various openings and connections trailing from the end of the other's words. Light bulbs go on in the brain, the hands move, self-consciousness goes by the board. You are no longer there to give and receive opinions, your coats are flying in the wind as you are pulled along by something as yet unsaid that you know is wanting to declare itself, even though you don't know what it is. It is an exercise of the heart and mind and, like physical exercise, its stretching leaves us rejuvenated, vivified, more connected to life and to meaning.

It is not always as easy as it sounds. I have just had a phone conversation with a friend in Switzerland, and I realized on putting the phone down that I had hardly heard a thing. After the first five minutes, my attention was distracted by a nagging concern over the cost of the call; not only that, I had an agenda. I was phoning to ask him a favour. I was wondering if he could help me locate some material I needed for this book. Though we had not spoken for a year or more, and there was much we had to exchange, my agenda was always on my mind. I was torn between the simple need for some information and the wish to engage in a dialogue with a friend. Our talk was amicable, even enjoyable. By the end, though, I felt that I had fallen between two stools, and done us both a subtle disservice. I had been unable to give him my ear.

A good conversation generates a relationship, a momentum and a dynamic that can take the participants further in some way than they were before. For such a relationship to occur, there cannot be a utilitarian agenda. When we strike deals, however friendly we are, we are bartering. Bartering introduces a relationship of a different kind. It can be fun, and it has its own skills, not least of which are the bluff and the waiting game. Bartering can test your mettle, but it is not conversation. Swapping information is something else again, a cerebral exchange from one memory bank to another. While a conversation will be informative, information is not its prime motivation. In fact, it may have little or no motivation at all, other than the sheer delight of engaging in a dance of heart and mind with the other person. This is one reason why it is so difficult to have a real conversation on the telephone. The telephone communicates information well enough, but with two disembodied voices trying to give the semblance of being together, it finds it far more difficult to communicate the person. It is hardly surprising, then, that the misunderstandings that occur on the phone are legion.

Conversation is expansive, and flourishes best in a context which parallels its nature. It arises while walking, or when on a slow boat, or a train. The word itself supposedly comes from turning back and forth with someone or something, walking up and down, and going over the same ground. When I asked Richard Lannoy, the artist, what his favourite place for a conversation was, he said the verandah. On a verandah, he said, one has one's back to the house, to all the daily concerns of everyday living, and one's gaze and thoughts can reflect on a wider, larger view. I have never had a conversation on a verandah, but I know what he means. I feel the same about the *terrasse* of a café: there, one is also looking out on to the larger world. And a café has an open informality that can encourage words to flow more easily than the more formal arrangement of a lunch or a dinner. At the same time, it is true that conversation is food, and the table is a natural setting for it.

What is needed for a conversation to begin anywhere is a certain intentionality, an attentiveness, and an abandon. Not the intention to obtain this or that, to display oneself in this light or that; not the intent to be in the right or the wrong, to be superior, inferior, wise or innocent, to impress or convince; no, the intention, the willingness, rather, to be there with this person in the first place. That is not always easy; often, we do not want to be where we are at all, and then no exchange can take place beyond social superficialities. We look away, or down at our watch, we shuffle our feet and wonder how we can make a polite exit. Then, if we are willing to be with this person, are we willing to wonder with them, to reflect and explore rather than give answers; to join with them in discovering something about ourselves or about life that we had not suspected before?

If so, then a conversation will already be under way. It will set off hidden and unforeseen connections and generate a mind that is larger than the individuals involved. It will turn in unexpected directions and always be larger than any idea we may have had about its direction and purpose. There will be a sense of anticipation that carries it along; it will be a live thing, with a life of its own that we feel bound to follow, abandon ourselves to.

I remember still a few conversations that I was part of fifteen and twenty years ago – not the words, but the aliveness of spirit. They were seminal, in the sense that a possibility, a window, was opened that had never been noticed before. Some invisible fluid was passed back and forth in the words and impregnated us with a fresh view of our lives. At stake was usually our own sense of truth at the time. In some way, the meaning of our existence was fermenting in the discussion, whatever the content might be. This is why we would feel so alive. This is why sexuality and intellect could seem so close. It seemed at times like making love with words. The emphasis, though, was neither emotional nor genital, but fundamentally creative in another way. Words can be creative not only through their eloquence or elegance but, more importantly, by generating possibilities. Words can open doors in the mind that we didn't even know were there, and pass a vital current between one person and another. Openness is central; it implies the question of the discussion is an open one, lived in the heart and the mind, and shared with the other in a mutual enjoyment of inquiry.

A more recent conversation I remember was with Lindsay Clarke, the novelist. Lindsay wrote *The Chymical Wedding*,[4] the only novel I have read in a decade that I was unable to put down. I started out with a vague agenda at this meeting, too. I was thinking of asking him to run a seminar for The Open Gate[5] on the imagination. We spent four hours together, punctuated by a solitary cup of tea, and we never got round to discussing the seminar. The to and fro of our conversation left me with the impression of a shared attitude towards the world. Everyone knows that listening in, attention to, a conversation can forge a friendship; and friendship begins when two or more people let each other in – when they let down the drawbridge and reveal a glimpse of their inner world.

That began to happen in another conversation I was in recently with Chloe, Rebecca (her nine-year-old daughter), and Yann (my sixteen-year-old son). One evening, we began telling each other what it was like to share a sense of family together only every other weekend. Rebecca told us how strange it was for her to move from the world of her father, where she lives during the week, to our world; how different the worlds were, and how difficult it was sometimes to move from one set of expectations and mode of interaction to another. Yann, however, was now enjoying the contrast, and the opportunity he had to live two different styles of life, one in the country with his mother, and another in the city with us. I told Rebecca how I loved her aliveness, and how sad I felt, too, at times, when she resisted enjoying herself in our company for fear, perhaps, of betraying her other life. It was an evening when we were all able to listen to each other, and through that conversation we were brought more intimately together. Listening can do that; and sometimes, in that togetherness, one can taste the presence of the wider circle of humanity, the way we are all irrevocably connected in a dimension greater than time.

This is the doorway to a different quality of conversation, in which a sense of presence supercedes the animation and intensity already described. The stillness that comes from being of one spirit descends without warning, an unexpected gift. As in any genuine conversation, the whole body comes alive. Listening, not thinking, in this bodily way, the appropriate words fall out of the mouth without anybody trying to do anything. Or there may be a silence for minutes on end. Yet we know, we can hear, that we are together, of one mind and heart. When one speaks, they are speaking for the other as well. The words could almost come out of anyone's mouth. It doesn't matter who says the words, and it barely matters, ultimately, what is said, since what is being exchanged and communicated is wordless. This is intimacy, the simplicity of shared being, through which we are most deeply restored. It is everything, and yet nothing to speak of, as all lovers know.

SILENCE

Imagine having no tongue. Being speechless. I know a man who chose not to speak more than twenty years ago, and has never uttered a word since. His name is Chandra Swami.[6] He is one of the most vital, radiant people I have ever met. When asked why he still keeps his vow after all this time, Chandra Swami writes that he has fallen in love with the silence. He no longer needs it as a discipline, but it remains a source of continuing joy. Now, twenty years might seem a little extreme, but falling in love with silence is common among religious people in all traditions; it is rare that it is felt as an imposition. The vow of silence is integral to the Carthusian Order of monks, and is usual for some period of the day in every religious order around the globe.

The reasons are simple. There is nothing in this world that proclaims the grandeur and beauty of life on earth more eloquently than silence. And then, in silence, we find out who we are. It is one of the greatest gifts we can offer ourselves; especially in a world that is thoroughly addicted to noise. Noise, rather than silence, is the opposite of sound. Silence, on the other hand, is the intensification of sound to its absolute essence.

It is as if we are afraid of silence. We seem desperate to fill every public corner and every occasion with what is rarely any more than an apology for music – muzak, drum machines, synthesized mindlessness. Lifts, shopping malls, hotel lobbies, airports – almost every public space is plastered with a thick coating of musical mediocrity. It is rare to find a restaurant which does not inflict similar damage on its clientele; rare, even, to find one that plays music which enhances the food rather than making it indigestible. Even without the muzak, the contemporary world is fraught with a daily babble: torrents of words that cascade around every building and over every garden fence. In her novel, *Oranges Are Not The Only Fruit*,[7] Jeannette Winterson comes up with an inventive, if partial, solution. She has a sky-cleaner come on duty every night and mop up all the verbal flotsam and jetsam that is floating over the city. We would do better, though, to address the cause. Imagine what it would be like in Paris or New York if, even for ten minutes a day, everyone went about their business without speaking.

A wonderful thought, though it will never happen – chattering is just too much of a habit for us all to break. Why do we gossip and chatter ourselves silly? There is ordinary human warmth in it, the wish to communicate without really knowing what to say; without knowing how to be together in silence. There are the nothings we say which simply mean 'We're here together, in this together', waiting for the bus, at the next table in a café, an expression of human solidarity and friendliness in a shared shower of rain. And there are the semi-articulate gropings which are trying to express interest, trying to tell a person you want to know who they are.

We all know, though, how these innocent exchanges can go on far longer than needed to share the benevolence of human warmth. So many words we use have an underbelly of emptiness, a chill, even, as if they were some frenetic attempt to stave off our own loneliness, our anxieties, the vacuum we feel, perhaps, just behind our own comforts, behind our own bedside lamp, or behind our words.

No amount of words or piped music will ward off the demon of emptiness indefinitely. The only way, as with all dragons, is to turn and face it. To sit there in the silence, defenceless except for the sword of attention; attention to the silence itself. The emptiness, the loneliness, will fade like mist in the sun before that sword, if only we don't let it fall. Sitting in silence – not meditating, not doing anything other than sitting wherever we happen to be, and listening – we would discover that, far from becoming engulfed, the world would come alive in our ears, and we would come alive to ourselves. We would realize there is a lot to be said for not speaking every now and then. We would feel sympathy with Wordsworth who, in the first of four sonnets he called 'Personal Talk', wrote:

> I am not One who much or oft delight
> To season my fireside with personal talk . . .
> Better than such discourse doth silence long . . .
> To sit without emotion, hope, or aim,
> In the loved presence of my cottage fire
> And listen to the flapping of the flame
> Or kettle whispering its faint undersong . . . [8]

We would be able to listen, too, to other people's voices instead of our own. We would perceive the city in new ways: its living soul would speak. Its main thoroughfare would no longer be a way to get somewhere, it would be the city's pulse, which we could feel beneath our feet. Our local café would be the matrix of the city's business, its love affairs and dreams, not just somewhere to jerk us awake with some caffeine.

After a few hours of silence, we ourselves will have a different sound. The energy and life that we normally disperse in a day's worth of words would still be circulating in our body. We would be gathered, contained, more present to ourselves than if we had flung words over our friends like confetti. We would begin to sense the weight of words, how potent they can be, and how wise it is not to waste them. Our own speaking, after an interim of silence, can carry our true meaning more easily. It will have a tone, a stillness, that will make others happy to listen. It will remind them, and us, that what we say, and how we say it, matters; for words collect over cities, over whole countries, and touch the minds of generations. Just as even now we may be voicing the thoughts of ancestors we never knew.

$\mathscr{I}$NTERIOR $\mathscr{E}$CHOES

Sitting in my room listening to the sound of the distant traffic, the creaking of the gas fire, the pregnant feel of the air in the room, I suddenly feel on the verge of tears. How deep into the interior dare I tilt my ear? In the same way I might listen for essence of river in the slap of lazy wave against a downstream spur of sand. At the mere thought, tears have sprung, and melancholy echoes begin to whisper a sadness around the edges of my body. I shudder slightly in recognition, the echoes already fading.

This sadness, sweet, is the living breath of stones and plants, of wind and rain, fox and badger, just as it is of us. What is the sound of sobbing? Earlier today, I passed a couple leading their child out of the psychiatric care unit. She was kicking and screaming, refusing to cross the road. Her screams ripped into my body, along with the anguish of her parents, and I bent double over my bike and pedalled faster. That scream was a sobbing turned sour.

In the melancholic chorus that has just faded away in my

room, there was a faint but distinguishable base line of sobs; long, slow, wholly unapologetic and unindulgent sobs. 'I surrender, I surrender', that's what they were singing. 'I can do no more, I can hear no more, I have nothing left, this is my darkest hour.' Lord of Life, give me the ears to let these voices in, let them pour through my body, release them from the dark interiors they have been clamouring in for so long, my spleen, my liver, the forgotten reaches of my half-used lungs. This sobbing, everywhere to be heard beneath all the world's smiles and presentable faces, will go on longer than we will, forever ready to moisten with its dark waters our deserts and barren regions.

Today there is a wildness in me that wants to twist and turn and sing for all it is worth. This song, though, wants to come out in words that make no sense, crazy words, unutterable even in their entirety. They spurt out in vowels half-begun and consonants that falter before the next syllable. Chaaa! Whaaa! Spilling over, sound spilling over a heaving chest churning and chafing at the bit and pouring in fountains from all my orifices. Burning white hot sounds but so tiny so minuscule so fine of vibration they are not for the ordinary ear to hear.

Their echo, even so, lingers on, and impresses on my mind with an indubitable stamp that *the gates are open the lid is off the genie is out of the bottle the skeletons out of the cupboard the ghost is out from behind the door of orderly sensitive reason.*

It comes so softly, the night in England, as if a thousand lights are turned off one at a time. I love the enveloping dark. It brings with it the departure of the raucous gull and the final mutterings of the city pigeons that gather for their last consultation on the chimneypots across from my bedroom window. It brings with it a gathering of my senses, a return to some closer intimation of myself that the day had disguised in all manner of outer doings.

Projects, ideas, the necessities of everyday living, fade away on the soft sound of a sigh falling from my own lips. I like to think that sigh is the breath of life in me. The pipes are in that sigh, the reed pipes that mountain people play to keep themselves company on their way home. Bittersweet sadness, beyond the telling. Even this sound, though, as I follow it, goes the way of all sounds and trails off into a vast empty space that is brimming with silence.

The darkening sky, a resounding bell, shudders the air in my room, its shadows falling over my face and desk. I hesitate to turn on my lamp as the last glint of day is sucked into the ocean of descending darkness. Can I withstand the gathering crescendo, or will this irresistible embrace call forth a new life? Just under my tongue, beneath my breath, the dark womb of Being lives, silent and startling. It coaxes me to lean back: 'Fall into my vastness and lose your grip. I am the sound you long to hear, deeper than any night, longer than any day, closer to you than all your lamentations and celebrations. Closer to you than your own heart. It is I who sing the stars into being.'

$\mathscr{B}$EING $\mathscr{H}$EARD

Strange to think that a flow of air has only to pass over a band of striated muscle for a person's soul to be revealed. That, however, is the way of it. We put our ear against a person's heart when we listen deeply to the sound of their voice. Jacques Lusseyrand confirms this in his book *And There Was Light*.[9] Lusseyrand became one of the leaders of the French Resistance in the Second World War while still in his teens. Suspected agents or informers for the Nazis were always brought to him for an interview. He was blind, and because his hearing was consequently so acute, he could immediately tell if they were telling the truth or not. Frankie Armstrong, the blind singer, says she can always tell from the sound of a person whether they are to be trusted. She was walking home in London one night when she heard some footsteps behind her. Though she had often walked home before, this time she sensed danger, and quickened her pace. The footsteps behind her quickened as well, and on the spur of the moment she turned round and faced the stranger with a bloodcurdling cry. He immediately turned and ran.

Even our footsteps, then, can speak to sensitive ears. We do not need to be blind, though, to listen more deeply to the people around us. Neither does listening need to be our profession, as it is for counsellors and therapists, in order for us to hear other people. It is an activity we all have the equipment for; it is a question of the time and the inclination. To lend an ear is the most natural form of empathy, of 'feeling with' someone; and our ears open to the degree we are willing to let our judging mind go and to give our attention to the person we are with. Listening to another can lead to an intimate exchange of our most tender, inarticulate thoughts. When this happens, we are swimming in the same current as the other; not standing back at a certain distance, but rolling and curving with them in the same wave. This kind of listening draws people out from beneath the surface world; it enables them to find words for the inexpressible. And yet it is not remotely manipulative – in fact, no one is doing anything at all – the whole interaction is revealing itself to both speaker and listener as it unfolds. As soon as self-consciousness comes in, as soon as there is someone busy being 'a listener', this deeper listening fades away.

So real listening is less an activity of the conscious mind than an intuitive faculty of a more ancient region of the brain, the remnant of a time when we swam like fishes in the shared plasma of life. The most remarkable listener I have ever heard of is Momo. She is the main character of Michael Ende's book, *Momo*.

She listened in a way that made slow-witted people have
flashes of inspiration. It wasn't that she actually said any-

*thing or asked questions that put such ideas into their
heads. She simply sat there and listened with the utmost
attention and sympathy, fixing them with her big dark
eyes, and they suddenly became aware of ideas whose
existence they had never suspected. Momo could listen in
such a way that worried and indecisive people knew their
own minds from one moment to the next, or shy people felt
suddenly confident and at ease, or downhearted people felt
happy and hopeful.*[10]

On one occasion,

*a little boy brought her his canary because it wouldn't
sing. Momo found that a harder proposition. She had to
sit and listen to the bird for a whole week before it started
to trill and warble again.*[11]

We start where we are: we listen to the words people use,
the weight and tone they give them, the speed of delivery,
the slur or the precision of language, the body posture that
accompanies the sentences. We give our interest; we notice
if we are feeling seduced, or humoured, or preached at. We
listen for where the words have come from in the body –
from the belly, perhaps, or the chest; or perhaps the sound
is a nasal one. Each origin carries its own quality, vital, emotional, or intellectual, and the more we listen, the more we
will be in tune: when we speak, our own voice may adopt a
similar tone and timbre to theirs; our posture and gestures
will harmonize, and the exchange will become a dance that
dances itself. Then, whatever we hear, we will always be en-

couraged to listen for more, knowing that the voice reaches down deep into the person.

Listening to a person's voice, it is not only the words that we hear. Underneath their words, and in their silences, people speak louder than ever. Sometimes, we sit talking with someone about some trivial affair, and we know that our gossip is only obscuring a deeper call for help, for understanding, companionship, or for the simple need to be held in another's arms. Or we may be talking great ideas, high philosophy, and know all the time that beneath our excited words there is another voice that is crying in a wilderness, lost and not knowing which way to turn. In a context of genuine listening, these subterranean voices can feel safe to emerge into the light and pass on their way. Listening itself is a healing practice, for the listener as well as the speaker. Ram Dass tells how he was giving a lecture one night when a man in a suit and tie stood up to ask a lengthy and convoluted question. Ram Dass could not hear a word, even though the amplification was perfectly clear. All he could see was this fish, a gasping mouth begging for some affirmation. When the fish had finished asking his question, Ram Dass was silent for a moment, at a loss for words, and then spontaneously found himself saying, 'I love you.'[12]

How often have we really been heard in our lives? To be wholly listened to is one of the greatest affirmations we can receive. It is rare; it is to be recognized, remembered, reminded that we have a place, a value, a right to be alive – not for what we do, for what we have done or are going to do, but for who we are, for the person that we ourselves may never have heard.

Those who most need us to hear them are our children, and from a very young age. Not being heard or seen – not being recognized – makes it difficult (the English psychologist, D.W. Winnicott,[13] would have said impossible) to hear or recognize ourselves; to have a sense of our own identity and place in the world. Children grow before our eyes in the light of a loving attention. I know the sadness, my own as well as his, of all the occasions when I have not listened to my own son. Not through malice, or intentional neglect, but through the more subtle unconsciousness that accompanies an absorbed self-concern. I do not say this as a confession of guilt, but because it is part of the truth. It is also true that his strengths, his vulnerabilities, his insight and beauty, have burst through my self-absorption at times and made me sit up and listen with a love and attention that have nourished us both, and shown me how little of my listening heart I often use.

Voices Ancient and Modern

In the West we are hearing the rhythmical voice again in one of its most ancient of forms: storytelling is enjoying a revival, perhaps because we are hungry to listen, because we long to be moved. I once watched a storyteller at work in the central square in Marrakesh, Morocco. I had no idea what he was saying, but I was rooted to the spot by the cadences of his voice. I was drawn into the rapt attention of his audience, who were like the snake of the snake charmer at the other end of the square. They moved as one to the sound of the storyteller's voice, gently this way, then that, craning forwards as he fell into a whisper, backwards when he leapt into a roar.

Robert Bly[14] is a Western equivalent. He has a voice of gravel which he accompanies with an out-of-tune balalaika. He is a showman, a good one. He usually precedes a recital by telling the audience that he likes to repeat his lines. This, he says, is because a first reading usually goes down no deeper than the listener's neck; a second reading reaches into the chest, and the third will finally land in the belly. What he says, the stories he tells, the poems he recites, enter the bones of the audience, and are repeated and passed on from coast to coast. His secret, I think, is that he acts himself. He and Gioia Timpanelli in New York, Michael Meade in Washington, and many others, are reviving the oral tradition and the listening ear that goes with it. Michael Meade presses the words home with a drum. He never tells a story without beating those congas, and every body and soul in the room taps and sways as the story unfolds.

The radio has probably done more than any other

medium this century to sustain an interest in storytelling and the human voice. More people hear poetry on B.B.C. Radio in one evening than in all the combined live poetry readings in a year in Britain. What the listener loses by not being in company, and in the direct presence of the performer, he gains in the influx of poetry into his own everyday context. Words well placed and spoken on a radio can change the mood or direction of the day itself. The most memorable radio voice I know is still the leisurely sound of John Arlott. He happens to have been a cricket commentator, but I would not have minded if he had talked about cookery, gardening, or the stock exchange. Cricket does have a more leisurely pace than other competitive sports, and it continues to appeal to a wide audience. But I am not among that number. It was not cricket that made me tune into John Arlott, it was his voice. It came predominantly from his chest, a resonant, open-hearted sound, its roots in the West Country of England rather than in the clipped and starched Oxford English of other B.B.C. voices of his generation. His tone evoked a slower, gentler age, and a warm, friendly masculinity embedded in secure and living traditions. John Arlott's England has almost faded away, even though cricket is played as always on the village green; but some of its qualities live on in that melodious voice, to be heard now only in the B.B.C. sound archives, or in the private memories of the millions who appreciated him.

One of the attractions of John Arlott's voice was its

accent, a West Country drawl that curled one word into the next. An accent has roots. It is tied to a particular part of the earth and proclaims a degree of belonging to a local community. Far from being consciously sculpted, a local accent and turn of phrase grow organically out of their surroundings; they carry the history of a place and the character of its people in their tone and inflections. A Scot has a quality of soul whose flinty character echoes in the sound of his voice, so different to the soft lilt of Irish. The Northumbrian strikes a different note to the Yorkshireman, while a Devonian evokes on his soft, rolling tongue another caste of mind to them all. Listen to the opening lines of *Twenty Years A-Growing*, a marvellous autobiography of a man brought up in the lyrical folk tradition of Western Ireland around the turn of the century. The original was written in Gaelic, but the vigour and grace of the language survive the translation:

> *There is no doubt but youth is a fine thing though my own is not over yet and wisdom comes with age . . . I remember well, when I was four years old, I was in the town of Dingle in the care of a stranger woman, because I was only half a year old when my mother died, dear God bless her soul and the souls of the dead. So there was no one to take care of me. I had two brothers and two sisters, but at that time they had little more sense than myself. So, as I have said, my father sent me to Dingle to be cared for by a woman there.*[15]

This is English written as if it were being spoken. The

rhythm and inflection could only ever come from Ireland. Local distinctions, as well as the different sounds of our national languages, are part of our given inheritance. They contribute to the raw material out of which we shape our thoughts and forge our individual personality.

Yet the voice reaches down deeper than this; deeper than any individual mark altogether, especially when it is sung. The singing voice can cross all boundaries of nationality and language and bring people together who might seem to have nothing in common. Something in the high nasal note of the Ethiopian singer, Aster Aweke,[16] enters the white bodies of many British and American people and strikes them to the core. So does the sound of the Bulgarian women of the Trio Bulgaka,[17] even though no one understands a word they sing. Of all the voices I have ever heard, though, the one that returns me to myself more than any other is that of the muezzin in the minaret, calling the faithful to prayer. Many voices are more beautiful, more soothing, more elevating, even; but this is a strident, plaintive call from beyond the ordinary pleasures and pains of this world, a call to come home, whoever we are.

What is it then, this power of the voice to reach down deep and turn us around? It is the power of being. The voice is 'the muscle of the soul'. It can embody and express the heights and depths of human experience. This must be why Mohammed chose it to call his people to prayer.

ℱAMILIAR 𝒱OICES

My mother met my father when she was barely nineteen and he was in his mid-thirties. For fifty years, she devoted her life to her marriage and children. She is one of the happier people I have known; but now he has died, she can hear that she still has the voice of the girl that she was. She has a lot of living to do. She brims with excitement and interest over a new book, a journey, a foreign language to learn. At other times her words are clipped, barely able to squeeze through lips too tightly held, restraining feelings she is afraid or embarrassed to express; or voicing only a whisper of some dream too big for her body. On her walls she has hung paintings of women leaning out of windows. A voice sensible, tamed by reason and the restraint of her day; yet tinged maroon with an unquenched fire, which gives her cautious words an undertow of barely concealed derring-do.

My father's voice was slow and considered, full like an apple just fallen from the tree. And yet, shy like a young man afraid of his love. Not many words would slip out at a time, but when they did they would start in his belly and ripple up through his chest. His tones would rarely rise or fall beyond the limits his own youth must have set; limits which, when reached, would sound a sullen chord, resigned, as if the life had been beaten back in him. In the last week of his life I heard unapologetic affection in his voice, though for years I had recognized it in the cast of his eyes as I came through the door.

It was by hearing a voice on the phone that I was led to the woman I love. It was Chloe's voice that, when I first heard it, sounded a bell in me. Even over the phone, her sonorous sound carried her whole body along with it, open and resonant from head to foot, a laughing, soulful, living sound, tumbling waters, a dreaming maiden and a wise old woman all in one voice. Now, after several years of living together, this voice is the one I still hear above all others, though deepened and strengthened now by some strong life-encounters. I have never heard bitterness in her, the twist of self-pity, or defeat. I have heard sadness, deep from her well, and the voice of gathering anger; and I have heard a strong, quiet sound that emerges from behind the shadow play of any social or cultural mask. She is a singer, and her singing awakens the ears to an echo of something faintly remembered, an open-throated calling to one's deeper dreams. There is an old spiritual which proclaims that 'part of me wants to sing about the light, and part of me wants to cry, cry, cry . . . ' Chloe's voice calls to both these voices in me at the same time, indistinguishable in their laughing/crying, crying/laughing.

$\mathcal{T}$HE $\mathcal{S}$PEAKING $\mathcal{W}$ORLD

Everything has its own sound, and speaks in a language known to its kind. We, who are immersed in this teeming world yet engrossed in our own affairs, have whole symphonies pass through us that, often, we do not even catch a note of – the orchestras of the birds, the whisperings of grasses, and sounds too subtle for our ears to register, like the low drone of stones and the high pitch of distant stars. Everything is calling out, hoping to be heard, and if we listen, we can hear voices from surprising directions.

I know a man who has even had a conversation with a lamp-post. You may call him crazy, but I am not so sure. It all started when he was walking down the street in an old part of London one day so immersed in his own thoughts that he walked into a lamp-post – one of those old ones which lean a graceful, wrought-iron arm over the pavement. Before he knew what he was saying, he was apologizing to it. That knock on the head had brought him awake to the reality of lamp-posts. This one was just standing there doing its job when he walked straight into its world. In that moment, that piece of metal came alive for him, and spoke with a voice of its own.

There is another true story, about a speaking tree, that has been passed down in India since the time of Alexander the Great. When Alexander reached northern India, he gathered together the wise men of the area and asked which of the many marvels of the country he should visit. They all recommended the Speaking Tree, which announced to the inquirer his destiny. When Alexander arrived there he beheld a huge deodara tree with many women, dressed in bright and various colours, sitting in its branches. When he reached the foot of the tree it declared that if he entered with his troops any deeper into India, he would never leave the country alive. Alexander disregarded the warning, forged into the country with his army, and never returned.[18]

There is another story from India which grew out of my own life. It is about a living river. We were staying in the tourist bungalow on the banks of the Ganges at Hardwar. The door of our room was open and we could hear the rush of the river outside. As we were sitting there, watching the day, the cleaner crept in with his brown reed-brush. He was stooped, older than his years, a sad little man. We were prompted to ask if he had a family. 'Yes,' he said; and then after a pause, 'but my wife is ill and my child too. We have no money for medicines; this is very difficult time.' He spoke entirely without guile; without the slightest suggestion that we should give him money. He was just stating the facts of his life. He made to start his work and then, as if remembering something, he turned and pointed through the doorway to the river. 'But Ma Ganga will take care of us,' he said. 'We live by Ganga, and she will take care of us.' Without another word, he carried on sweeping the floor. I had never heard anyone talk about a river in that way before. The Ganges was, for him, a living river, a protector, a healer of ills and a bestower of blessings.

In Europe, too, before the Age of Reason and Enlightenment began to sweep away all voices except that of the rational mind, the rivers, the stones, the mountains spoke. Human beings were in a vital relationship with the living world. The world of Nature was – and still is, if we look and listen – the feminine face of God, the fusion of matter and spirit. There was once a sage in India whose only spiritual practice was to listen to the waterfall he lived by and to constantly sing its praises. 'How beautiful, how beautiful you are,' was his only mantra.

Now it is true that he might have found it more difficult with a lamp-post. Our world in the West is crammed with man-made things more than with the beauties of Nature. Nature is an inspiration for most people at one time or another, and it speaks to us loudly as children. Wordsworth thought that Nature was a necessary second mother for the pre-adolescent child, and if that relationship was missing, the child's imagination would be stunted in some way in later life. Imagination feeds on old tree roots, the smell of wet grass, and the shimmer of corn in the sun.

We need, then, to go out and listen to the wind, to shudder at the power of some old standing stone; we need to receive the blessing – the look, the touch, the voice – of Nature. But there is more: we need to pass that blessing on to the things that inhabit our world; to the hissing kettle, that old car, the creaking bathtub, the city street, the ugly and the irritating as well as the beautiful; yes, even the telephone deserves our attention. To give attention to something is to listen to it, to acknowledge its value and presence in the world. This is what Salman Rushdie is referring to when he speaks of his childhood:

> *I grew up kissing books and bread. In our house, whenever anyone dropped a book or let fall a chapati . . . the fallen object was required not only to be picked up but also kissed, by way of apology for the act of clumsy disrespect. Devout households in India often contained, and still contain, persons in the habit of kissing holy books. But we kissed everything. If I'd ever dropped the telephone directory I'd have probably kissed that too. Bread and books: food for the body and food for the soul – what could be more worthy of our respect than that?*[19]

Attention is the blessing we have to give, as the young Rushdie grew to learn – after much kissing, he freely admits, of dictionaries, atlases, Enid Blyton novels, and even Superman comics. Neither Nature nor our possessions need our sentimentality, our fantasies of what we think they are, our pseudo-spiritual need for them to assume the meaning that we may have lost in ourselves. No, they need us to listen to them for a change, so that they might speak to us in their own way and communicate their own inherent worthiness of respect.

I have already disclosed a certain disaffection I used to feel for the telephone. It is difficult to hear anything or anyone if we are besotted with our own attraction or aversion for them. Thich Nhat Hanh freed me of my dislike of the phone. Tai, as he is known, is a Vietnamese monk, a Buddhist, living in France. He says the best way to come to value the phone is to listen attentively to three rings before picking it up, while being aware of one's breathing. Listening makes friends, and honours the life in others.

It is a small act, to wait and listen before answering the phone, but it changes things. My relationship to that everyday humdrum activity is no longer the same. The way we learn to feel the life of the world is to start small; to listen to a friendly voice, like the wind or the rain, or the kettle, perhaps; to one of the voices we hear all the time but never give the time of day to. If we give the things of our world the benefit of the doubt, the hint that they might be worth listening to, then who knows, no promises, but life, startled by our sudden interest, may speak to us from the most unlikely of quarters. We may be walking up Fifth Avenue, or stepping on to the tube in London, and suddenly everything, the people, the buses, the buildings, the platform, the train, the lights, may all erupt in a chorus, a multi-part choir that has been singing for centuries but we have only just heard. We have to start small, though, with a few regular moments of attention to the sound of the cat purring, the phone ringing, or the doorbell. The rest we can leave to life.

We may imagine that the world only ever comes alive when we turn to it. No, life has been watching and listening to us since the day we were born. We come alive, present to ourselves and to life, when we turn to it – it has never stopped breathing, listening, and watching for an instant. We have so lovingly constructed an anthropocentric world since the Renaissance, so entirely filled the forms of life with our own dreams, fantasies, and projections, that it has now become a feat of the imagination to suspect that living things may have an existence independent of ours. We are all rising and falling within the parameters of the same four elements, of course; we all share the same breath, and our dreams and our thoughts pass in and out of each other. At the same time, we – humans, animals, rocks, and plants – stand, in varying degrees, alone, with our own fate and destiny.

As for the things that have sprung from the mind of man, it is true that theirs is a different life. The cups and plates in the kitchen, the old sofa, the piano, the laptop computer, theirs is a reflected light; a reflection not only of the mind of their maker, but of all the dreams and fears we have had in their presence. The sofa carries the echoes of every whisper made upon its seat: every lie told there, and every loving thought, is breathing still in its back and arms. On a larger scale we all know this well. We feel the cumulative intensity of the devout in a cathedral, collected like dew over hundreds of years.

Everywhere the past speaks on into the present. Last

Wednesday I walked across the Clifton Downs in Bristol. In the distance was the familiar rumble of traffic and the occasional outburst of a horn. I suddenly sensed how different it was a hundred years ago: the clatter of hooves and wooden wheels on cobble, and just every now and then the odd shout or cry losing itself in a quieter sky. Nothing lost, though; those cries echo still across the bridge, and filter in between the words we use.

$\mathcal{A}$LL $\mathcal{E}$ARS

One day, in Devon, beside the river Dart, Chloe led me, blindfold, for a walk over the hills. It is a warm thing, to be led, to be in trust, entrusted to another. I immediately heard the sheep bleating over the combe, where an instant before only our own voices had filled my ears. In the same moment, I could hear the rooks rustling in the treetops far above our heads. We were passing through a beech wood, and the beechnuts were crunching under our feet. More than anything else, though, and within a few minutes, I felt the relief of being returned to my own body. Our eyes usually take us away from ourselves, and absorb our attention in some external concern. Without eyes, I remembered that I, too, am a warm thing, full of sensations, with feet treading a path that has always been there for them. I am a breathing creature whose flesh softens as soon as the intent and direction of the eyes is removed.

With my ears replacing my eyes as my primary sense, I was no longer forging forwards; instead, I was increasingly aware of living and moving in circular space. There was no longer any need to rush, since I was no longer going anywhere in particular. No longer living for the front view alone, no longer having a face to put on, my back and my sides came alive with ears of their own and I began to hear from all directions at once. The hooting of the ferry far out in the estuary; the beating of wings filling the sky above my head; my own breath, heaving a little as we climbed up the hill and out of the woods; a chugging tractor somewhere; and the oozing of our footsteps on the soft, wet clay: everything everywhere formed a mosaic of sound in which we were included as elements among others in the harmonies of life.

When Chloe spoke, the sound of her words entered me without resistance from the judging or discursive parts of my mind. I just listened, and took her in whole on the waves of the wind. It is a relief, to listen to another when the protecting veils have fallen away. Far in the distance a siren wailed, a police car or an ambulance, perhaps, reminding me of the trouble we get ourselves in. I was not troubled there, in the dark of my body as it climbed the combe. My thoughts had slowed to a walking pace, and I could hear the stillness in the afternoon air. Neither was I concerned when a bee, doing what bees do, circled my head in a buzzing fit, before dashing off to find someone else to quarrel with. The plod of our feet still rose from the mud; and the wind lifted a little, stirring the leaves in the oak tree that stood by the stile. The stile itself creaked a tired welcome as we climbed over it and made for the village on the other side of the hill. My ears had restored me to my proper proportion in the round of things. For a time, my ordinary perspective had been taken away, my distance from others dissolved, and I was returned to the community of the living earth.

Ocean Sounds

The whole western flank of Mexico shudders at the persistent pounding of Pacific rollers. There the engine of wind and the tireless, unceasing labour of water against rock produces a primordial, deep-throated booming. It sounds like the birth of the world. This ocean's voice is abandoned to itself, utterly released and surrendered to the necessity of its fate. It is rolling, naked, laughing freedom, an echo of my own ecstatic life that I know somewhere in my marrow; that I have closeted deep behind the carapace that I pretend is me, while knowing all the time it is not.

Emphatic, persistent, without the slightest self-doubt, she bursts through the circus of sounds in our worried heads. Why should she worry? She dances lightly on the bones of a million men. She knows no pity for faltering souls. And yet she is rest, deep repose, endless compassion. Teeming life and irrevocable death in the curl of a single wave. Her sound can be none other than our own. We, too, are blown through with the same voice that speaks on the shore, and even hums a low, low murmuring, too low for our ordinary ears, in the rocks and the stones and the still mountainside. Somewhere in the heart of the crashing wave, at the heart of the listening human, is a sound so delicate and constant it is almost unbearable to hear. It is utmost ecstasy, and beckons our dissolution. In India, musicians have always spoken of *anahata*, the nameless sound within every sound. Few sounds can draw us more closely to it than the voice of the ocean, and my legs have been trembling gently now for an hour or more.

THE FOOD OF LOVE

Musically speaking, I consider myself to be little more than a borderline illiterate. Certainly, I am no more familiar with music than the average man in the street. Not, though, because the commercial music industry has hypnotized me with its thumping drumbeats, and galvanized my taste solely to the arousal of my gonads; and not because I have no interest in music. No, quite honestly, the main reason is that I prefer silence. I find background music, almost without exception, an intrusion which dulls my senses. When I am on my own, in my room, I will tend to pick up a book rather than put on a tape, though sometimes I will dance to something that lifts my step. The car and the motorway have become, for me, my principal concert hall. There, I can sing out loud, and let myself be transported.

Not often, though, by Brahms or Mozart, or classical music in general, and rarely by rock or pop. What I want from music is to be moved – to have the subtler degrees of my life awakened; to be stirred in body and soul, and returned to my senses, more alive to myself than before. Some classical music certainly does all these things. Fauré's *Requiem* never fails to move me; neither does Vivaldi's *Four Seasons*, Handel's *Messiah*, the music of Bach, Albinoni, Poulenc, and others – everyone has their personal preferences. But broadly speaking, classical music seems to strike my intellect more than the intelligence of the heart; and more often than not, it leaves my body behind.

Only recently, I have begun to realize why I may feel this way. It was only with the advent of Classical music in the eighteenth century that composers really took centre stage from performers. Composers *wrote* their music, to be *read* by the musicians. With Classical music, the eye began to gain sway over the ear. Musicians followed the logical sequence of separate notes with their eye instead of learning a piece 'by heart' and by ear. By the first method, the music enters the musician via the brain; by the second, via the foot-tapping, swaying body.

My preferred music is pre-Classical; contemporary music that is largely improvisational; and the music of certain oral cultures. Plainsong, Gregorian Chant, William Byrd; the blues, and a little rock music (both these forms have largely relinquished notation and rely instead on improvisation.) But even more, the traditional music of Persia, North Africa, and Southern Spain. When, in the sixties, everyone else was listening to Pink Floyd, The Incredible String Band, Jethro Tull, and all the rest, I was in another room listening over and over again to three or four records put out on a French label. At that time, the French seemed to be the only Europeans who were recording traditional music from oral cultures. Now, of course, it is known everywhere under the catch phrase of 'world music'.

This traditional music has deep soul, but not of the Negro spiritual kind. It sings not so much of unrequited love, poverty and disappointment, but rather of dreams and laments that speak for the whole community in its perennial dealings with both the gods and the earthly seasons. Often, the music is choral. The musicians are not a people in exile, but members of great and ancient cultures who have lived on the same land for centuries, and whose community life is deeply embedded in a spiritual sensitivity. Not only soul, then, but spirit breathes through their music. The cycle of the seasons takes place within a larger world view, which in its turn is rooted in the daily labours of trader, farmer, and herdman. In almost every example of music of this kind, from anywhere in the world, soul and spirit are personified by the melody on the one hand, and a constant drone on the other. The drone instrument, whether it be the tambura in

India, the didgeridoo in aboriginal Australia, or the bagpipes in Europe, represents the unchanging world of spirit within the dancing world of form.

The interplay of soul and spirit in this way is not the preserve of traditional cultures alone: some of the more inspired examples are now emerging from the meeting of traditional music and contemporary Western forms, and musicians from a variety of races improvising together on the same stage. The real point is that, for my part, music of this kind resounds in my chest and belly; it brings tears to my eyes, it alerts my senses, and makes me want to sing with joy. Above all, it awakens my mind and ear to a dimension that, in the midst of life's hopes and fears, sets the world aright.

For is not music the great healing balm, the food of love, the descent of heaven to earth? Has it not, since time immemorial, put flight to staid reason, uplifted broken souls, and touched the hearts of devout and unbelieving alike with an ecstasy more proper to the gods? It was Homer who boasted that his warriors could ward off the plague with their choral singing; David, on the testimony of scripture, who spirited away Saul's mental derangement with his harp. A modern harpist, Thérèse Schroeder, has opened a large centre in the United States, funded by medical practitioners, to ease the cancer patient's transition through death with specific pieces of music from the Middle Ages.[20] In Paris, the Tomatis Centre[21] uses music (primarily Mozart, which shows how subjective my own predilections are) to heal psychological disorders. Professor Alfred Tomatis, who has spent a lifetime in research on the effects of music, has also discovered that if music of a certain kind is played regularly to pregnant mothers, their children will be instantly soothed when the same music is played to them in times of distress.

Music is highly potent, both for good and for ill. Both Plato and Aristotle suggested that certain modes and instruments should be banned, because of their deleterious effects. In his sixteenth-century treatise, *De Musica*, (which was essential reading for a music degree right up to the middle of the last century), Boethius connected music with morality, and quoted Pythagoras as saying that the behaviour of a republic can have no greater stain than to abandon upright and honourable music.[22] Even making allowances for the high moral tone of a long-lost age, it does seem that a statement like that has something to say to our own era, with its remnants of punk, its heavy metal, its rap, and some of its more abstract, avant-garde experimentation. Certainly, we need to be selective in our choice of music, rather than accepting blandly the indiscriminate deluge of the popular media. We can make a point of asking the volume to be turned down in restaurants and public places where the music forced upon us is too obtrusive. Then, instead of having music as background 'company', we can give it the respect of either our full attention or of turning it off until we are ready to hear it.

Most people will say they prefer listening to music at home or in the car rather than going to a concert. With the aid of electronics, music has become a private experience, symbolized by the jogger running through a park with his headphones on; or you or me in our cars. The value of private music is far-reaching: it can deepen our subjective, interior world, helping us to explore more fully our higher and lower reaches; and it can inspire fresh insights into our life and direction. All this, quite apart from its obvious ability to create a desired mood or state of mind at will. Listening to live music has other qualities as well as these. In the first place, one is listening to something that is literally alive – it is spontaneous, open to error, a new event, subject to the particular conditions of the moment. There is always, in live music, a certain anticipation, an excitement that is not present in the same way when listening to recorded music that has been made as technically perfect as possible in the studio. Then, live music is a public event, something one shares with others. Few would dispute that the interaction of performers and audience can create an experience for every individual present that remains unknown to someone watching the same event on television.

I went to a live performance last year that I am unlikely ever to forget. It was in the Pump Rooms, in Bath. Hari Prasad[23] was playing, as part of the Bath Festival. Hari Prasad is India's most distinguished player of the wooden flute. Almost from the beginning, his body wound around the notes like a snake. The movements of his body and the extraordinary delicacy of his music were wholly intertwined. I had come to the concert feeling tired and heavy, but as it progressed I found myself being lifted into a state of aliveness and lightness that filled me with elation. It was as if the cells of my body had been stirred into a dance, and I could barely feel my weight on the seat. When I arrived home, quite late, I was too alive to sleep, and I listened to the tape I had bought of another of Hari Prasad's performances. When I finally lay down my body was as alive as ever, with my spine, especially, tingling lightly up the whole length of my back. I slept for a few hours and woke up far earlier than usual, far more awake than usual. It was not so much an emotional or intellectual influence that had acted on me, but rather a physical one. With his flute and his body, Hari Prasad had – this is the only way I can begin to describe it – altered the arrangement of my cells. Original magic. Music has that power.

$\mathcal{S}$EEING

When asked why he painted a picture of blue tomatoes, Matisse replied, 'Because I see them that way, and I cannot help it if no one else does. Take that table, for example,' pointing to one nearby, on which stood a jar of nasturtiums. 'I do not literally paint that table, but the emotion it produces upon me.'

Matisse[1]

$\mathcal{S}$IGHT $\mathcal{M}$EMORIES

a shoal of glistening fish in a pond squabbling over some crumbs

my father's slippers

the grey tin bath, a handle at either end, in front of the fire

a woman's body, white, so white, the first I had ever seen

my class, standing in line in the playground on my first day at
school, all with peaked caps and navy-blue blazers

two white cats, one with only one eye

rainbows in raindrops travelling along the telephone wire outside our
lavatory window

the steady gaze of my son, a few days old

the long dark hair and green eyes of a woman across a room when I
was eighteen

grey and white rocks elbowing their way out of hard red earth in
Provence

bulrushes nodding in the wind by a green pond in the woods

a kingfisher swooping across the River Avon

a grey, wet street in Brixton with nobody in it but me. I was five

the carcass of a goat among trails of flower offerings, mostly
marigolds, in the Ganges

three pigeons on a ledge, rustling their feathers

the sun rising, a burning red ball, over the purple Sahara

an old pine floor, stripped and varnished, in the kitchen

two red ants carrying a long white straw down a hole

a girl laughing at a bus stop

the gaping red split in a man's thigh after a motorcycle accident

emerald moss on a rock by a stream

the face of my beloved while making love

neatly piled skulls in the charnel house of a monastery on Mt Athos

THE AGE OF LIGHT

We live in a wholeheartedly visual society. The rule of optics is supreme. We can watch a microbe in an eyebrow, intestines digesting dinner, blood corpuscles in our veins. We can follow dolphins in the oceans, snow leopards in the Himalayas, and dust clouds in interstellar space. We can watch the earth rising over the moon. With night now thoroughly marginalized by the electric cable, we can get the view from every angle, twenty-four hours a day. The visual revolution has even gone so far as to suggest that the 'view' is preferable to the reality it represents. Boorstin tells a story about the contemporary suburban housewife 'who responds to a neighbour's compliment to her child with the boast: "Yes, he is lovely, but you should see the photograph".'[2]

The same revolution has switched image and reality back to front: images now precede the reality they are meant to represent. One might even say that reality has become a pale reflection of the image. When a little girl from London made her first visit to the country to stay with some friends of mine, they took her for a walk to introduce her to nature. When they paused to look over a gate at some cows, she wanted to keep walking. 'Seen them,' she said. The same happened with some sheep further along. Nothing was new to her, nothing held her attention, because she had already seen it on telly. Then there is the man in Bristol who has drawn some attention to himself for his unusual manner of birdwatching. He never uses binoculars, and never goes further than his living room, though he has seen varieties of birds from all over the world. He does his birdwatching in front of the television. He will watch the golf tournaments just for the chance flight of a heron across the green. On the nature programmes, it's not the lion in the foreground that interests him, but the little bird in the background that the commentator doesn't even mention. His greatest thrill is to identify that bird, which he can then tick off on his list as 'seen'. Why should he put on his gumboots and go plodding through country lanes when he can see far more in the comfort of his own home?

In a consumer culture, we should not be surprised that the image takes precedence over reality. The brand image and the packaging take precedence over the product because they are what sell. People buy images first, and products second. They buy images that correspond to, or substantiate, the image they have of themselves – or the image they would like to have of themselves. Public figures are maintained by our dreams and fantasies of them, which they play upon in order to keep their position. Politicians are an obvious example. They are elected on the media image they manage to convey. The media itself plays a duplicitous role by consolidating the politician's image on the one hand, and trying to puncture it on the other by uncovering some human feature that does not correspond with the image.

Since the voters vote for an image and not for a person, shock and disillusion break out if the frailties of a real person emerge from behind the idealized image. Either way, the media has a story, and the story is what counts, for we all love a yarn. We live less in a culture of production than of re-production; a world in which it is difficult to see anything fresh because we have already seen it in the adverts. Some of us do not even produce our own dream images any more: psychiatrists in the United States have noted that the dream images of many teenagers are lifted straight from the TV soaps. All those hours of living in a second-hand world of television, video, and computer graphics; all this peering into every nook and cranny with our optical wizardry; all this light thrown everywhere so that nothing can keep a secret – it puts a terrible strain on the eyes.

Our eyes have glazed over both from a surfeit of images, and from the effort of looking too hard. There are dozens of phrases to describe ways of seeing, but in the last half of this century, we have come down firmly in favour of two – sharp focus and rapid scan. The naked eye actually shifts focus between wide angle and telephoto about twenty times a second, though we see the image as fixed and centred in the field of vision.[3] The photographic image discounts these subtle movements and gives us one sharp image, 'better' than the real thing. The clearer and sharper the better – look at the fashion magazines and the television advertisements. The clarity we admire is dramatic and, above all, effective in its ability to stimulate our desire for the commodity. Desire is the cornerstone of consumer culture. To stimulate desire, we need to capture the market's attention and focus it on a particular product. To stand out among all the other products in the field, the product's packaging and promotion must catch the eye.

Photography, and especially television, have trained us to see at a glance the main features of an image. We can dart from one channel to the next, from one headline to another, like a computer in search mode, scanning the field for the information we want. We are in the age of collage, where television encourages everything – politics, the rainforest, a local tragedy, the Japanese stock market, art, pornography, comedy, dolphins, the late show – to vie for our attention at once, as if there were no difference in value to choose between them. Research in the United States has found that since the arrival of multi-channel press-button TV over fifty per cent of children under the age of fifteen have never watched an entire programme from start to finish.[4]

The speed at which we travel, too, has obliged us to snatch at a view and pass on to the next one. It is difficult not to see life as a series of film frames as we rush through the countryside in a train at 100 miles an hour; difficult, too, not to transpose that kind of 'rapid information glance' to the way we use our eyes in general. In a museum, people tend to pass by paintings as if they were walking to the buffet car and glancing out of the carriage window. It is easy to forget that it was not always like this. When Matisse was taken for automobile rides through the Provençal landscape, he would insist on speeds no greater than five kilometres an hour – a walking pace – 'otherwise, you have no sense of the trees.'[5]

In this age of light, in which nothing seems to be hidden from our eyes, we have lost sight of some of the most precious things of all. In the deluge of media images that veils the concrete world from our eyes, in our restless searching of the field with an acquisitive eye, we risk not seeing what is right under our nose. We do not see the living world. We do not notice the grapes over there in the bowl; we do not see the crumple of the blankets on our bed, the old shoe by the door, the stone wall. Over there is the front door, a blue one with an old bronze knob, not a brass one; and right here is my own right hand, moving across a blank white page. When did I last look at my own right hand? Or gaze on the face of the person I am living my life with?

Our desire for rapid-action focus, for clarity, immediacy, and information, has edged most other forms of seeing to the background. We glance still, for a glance is the sharp-shooter of the eye's arsenal. But in a fast-moving, homo-genized world, with only the most dramatic lines or events standing out here and there, it is rare that we find time to gaze, to reflect, to contemplate, or to behold. The slower, more considered uses of the eye have been largely swept from the board. After all, they serve no utilitarian purpose.

They can seem so out of place in contemporary life that they can even get you into trouble. Brian Skilton is a film maker. He told me that he was wandering down a London street one day looking up at the different houses. A police car stopped. Two constables got out and asked him what he was doing. 'I am interested in architecture,' he said, 'and I was just looking at these different houses.' 'Well, we are interested in looking at the way you are looking,' they replied. 'Nobody but a housebreaker would want to wander down a street looking up at houses like that.' In seeing only the surface of things, we can forget that there are more layers to life than one; that when seen with a slower, receptive gaze, visible form becomes a show of soul.

CLOSE-UPS

Yesterday I awoke and the horizon of my world was a fold in the duvet. The cover was hooded across my head and instead of looking immediately into the day, my eyes were content to rest on a zigzag of blue on a piece of cloth three inches from my nose. The cloth rolled away into a blur in the distance, like a great range of hills at the end of a warm day. Beyond the horizon, I knew it was otherwise – a cold morning in December; and I shuffled the mountain range so I could stay in its valleys. At such close quarters, a fold of cloth looms dauntingly large. I never knew a duvet could have such a presence. Perhaps it was because I had never

really looked at one before. Not that I was trying to look at it
then; it was just there, and so was I. Its proximity had
brought me up close to myself.

In another fold of the hills, a few inches away, I could
make out the flesh of my beloved's upper left arm. White,
with a flush of pink and brown, a beautiful tenderness.
Funny how freckles seem to gather together in clusters in an
ocean of white. I could not see where this hint of a human
being had come from, nor where it was going; only that it
was there, moist and humming with a large life of its own,
calling to the life that was living in me. I had no urge to
move from my bed that morning, with the world looming so
large at the end of my nose.

One of the many things that photography and film have
done is to bring faces very close to our eyes. We do not
afford ourselves the luxury of dwelling on real faces for long.
For one thing, people know very quickly that they are being
looked at, and we glance away as soon as they look up. We
usually construct our image of someone from a series of
rapid glances. Photography has allowed us to gaze on a person's face, or on a detail of their face, for as long as we wish.
With a full-length snapshot of a friend, especially if they are
in the middle distance, and surrounded by other figures and
landscape, we tend to pick it up and put it down. It is an
item of information more than anything else. Our distance
from it, our position as an outside observer, seems to bear

some relation to the distance the figure is from the fore-ground. The further away he is from us literally, the further away he seems metaphorically. In the same way, a close-up seems very close to us indeed – sometimes almost disturb-ingly close, as if we might be intruding on someone's private world. We would never normally be so close to that person as to be aware of the texture of their cheeks, the folds in their skin, the difference between the look in their left eye and their right. Yet it is not only the proximity of the physical person that gives us pause – the factual details of their appearance – but more our proximity to the soul that those details convey. In a close-up, a living soul is staring us right in the face, their suffering, their joy, their anxiety or their tranquillity plainly revealed. And in a gaze as undisguised as that, our own soul is stirred, and we, in turn, are brought up close to ourselves.

This is why close-ups can be so moving, and why they are consequently used with such effect on television to orchestrate our emotions. The honesty of a close-up evokes our conscience, that part of the soul which can sense the truth of things and acknowledge it. It is often used in charity appeals or on the news to evoke our sympathy for a Kurdish refugee or a bereaved woman in some civil war. It could helpfully be used more often on politicians, to help us see under their public face.

One of the finest close-ups available to us was completed nearly two hundred years before the first photograph was printed. It is the self-portrait painted by Rembrandt near the end of his life, in 1664. Earlier self-portraits had shown his more public face, such as the painting of himself with his first wife, Saskia, completed some thirty years before. That painting was executed in a formal, traditional style, like many of the portraits of its day. Its intent was primarily to show his happiness, prestige, and wealth, which was the reason paintings of this kind were routinely commissioned. The later self-portrait drops all pretence at a public face and puts the soul of the artist in the spotlight of the foreground, without anything else to detract the eye. An old man now, a lifetime's struggle gazes out on us from a face that is, even so, luminous with beauty and compassion. That gaze travels straight down inside me and stops me in my tracks. By having poured his soul on to that canvas, Rembrandt brings my heart into my mouth and faces me with the question of my own existence every time I bring myself to look upon it.

It is for that reason that it is worth getting up close to life. Even a duvet can surprise us if we are willing to take a closer look. How much truer that can be, then, of the face of an animal, or of a human being. That must be why it is so much harder to kill or injure another from close quarters, while looking in their eyes. In those eyes, our own fear, our own tragedy, our own love, is plainly revealed. The mirror of the world presents us with the face that is waiting to be recognized beneath our appearance, if only we will look.

REFLECTING ON EDGES

There is a Scandinavian restaurant in London, all black and white, whose designer has made an art of dwelling on the edges of things. Stark silver cutlery, no frills, stands out with neatly folded white napkins on sharp black tables, square ones, with clear-lined, stainless steel chairs arranged neatly around them. We like edges. They give tone and shape to form; they heighten our own definition, where we end and where the world begins. They accentuate our separateness and individuality. Push the edge and you meet with resistance, the certainty that something else lives and takes up as much space as you do, or perhaps more, and that you are going to have to negotiate for the space in the middle.

Different cultures have different notions of edges, and of what catches the eye. Nowhere is this more plain than in a city street. New Yorkers and Londoners are skilled pedestrians. They can rush down their crowded streets without even brushing anyone coming the other way. They have a built-in radar scanner that knows to weave this way rather than that even before the eyes have seen the space that they are already moving into. It is even a game to see how fast you can go without touching another person. Three hundred feet per minute is one estimate for an average walking speed on Fifth Avenue. People in large cities walk faster than people in small cities. Big-city dwellers are people on edge; they like to play the edge, walk right up to the edge and curve away at the very last moment. To play the edge, you don't think, you look, and you follow your nose. There is a lot of instinct along the edge. Stand on any street corner in central London, Paris, or New York. A street corner is one of the liveliest places in the modern world. The people who hang on a street corner are streetwise. They have an instinct for the street, and their eyes are everywhere, wheeling like gannets over a river, looking for the next opportunity – a likely customer, an untapped space in the market to fill.

In India, everything is different. Walk down a street in Delhi and people seem deliberately to walk into you. They don't see you. They don't see the empty space on your left. They are not looking. In New York, a pedestrian's eyes are everywhere, tracking a clear flight path twenty or thirty yards on down the pavement. In Delhi, you get pushed this way and that and nobody says a word. If you brush some-one's coat in the West, you apologize. If you have a head-on collision in Delhi, a local will walk on without looking twice. They do not have the same boundaries as we do. They have a strong awareness of social and caste differences, and main-tain those boundaries with a vigour that may seem unjust and misplaced to Westerners. Individual edges are less cru-cial to them. So everyone piles on top of each other. You are part of a crowd, one of a mass, so it is not a problem to crush five-deep into a railway carriage or a bus. Everyone merges into everyone else, on the street like anywhere else. It is even the same with the traffic. There are no white lines in the middle of the road. The whole thoroughfare is up for grabs, and you get by as well as you can. Often, you don't. Crumpled buses are a feature on the side of any Indian road. The motorcar is the product of a visual society that sees in straight lines; it makes a difficult transition to a world that has not yet made the leap from the oral tradition to the clarity that comes with perspective.

Our Western eyes, with their distance and objectivity, give us the edge when it comes to order and straight lines. They have given us the scientific method (science, from *scire*, to know through seeing); the square instead of the circle; they give us the different angles, the multi-party system, railway tracks and motorways; the street instead of the bazaar, sharp business suits instead of robes, office blocks of glass and steel, reflecting surfaces, and the double-edged sword of self-consciousness. Double-edged because in carving out our own space it runs the constant danger of cutting us off not only from each other but also from ourselves.

The people of India see differently. They do not see the edges we do, they see colour. They wear clothes that defy definition. The clothes of Indian women do not end abruptly somewhere above or below the knee; they flow on down to the ground, and even fan out behind them, merging them with their surroundings. They do not accentuate the shape of their body, they sensuously enfold it in colour and texture. Intense colour that is just not to be seen in the West:

oranges, blues, golds and yellows so breathtakingly vivid, so radiant, that they seem to be alive. And that is the point: their bodies are alive, whatever their shape; shimmering with a life unfettered by borders and conventions of shape and size. They present not only an image, but a brush of silk, a feel, a taste of a life lived more in the round, altogether more sensual and sensuous than the stark images of Western style. Yet it is the brilliant knack of our culture to draw together ideas and styles from around the globe and create something from them entirely new. There is an opening now for a coloured edge, a juxtaposition of Western focus and Eastern flow.

The Far View

Our gaze is normally fixed on the middle-ground of life, where all the action seems to be – a few yards up the street, or across the room. The other people in our lives usually occupy the safe distance of the middle-ground, within speaking range. This is especially true in the West, where we have a highly developed sense of personal space. It is not often, then, that we get to see life at close quarters; not often, either, that we manage to see the far view. Most of us live in cities where the farthest view is to the end of the street, and even that is usually obscured by our preoccupation with staying upright on the pavement, and out of the way of the traffic. Yet, like the close-up, which can bring us into intimate contact with ourselves, the far view can also be food for the soul, though in a rather different way.

Perhaps the far view that has been the most dramatic in human history to date is the one the American astronauts had of the Earth while standing on the moon. This image of the Earth rising is surely, of all views, the one that encourages – even demands – a change in the way the human race perceives itself. We can no longer, in the same way, lay claim to our uniqueness in the cosmos, or assert our separateness from each other. Like it or not, it is irrefutable, there for all to see, that all of us live on the same block, and that we share the duty of keeping our garden clean. That image places it beyond argument that we live on a beautiful, though delicate, ball, whose life is in our hands. The perception of a global community was ushered in with that single view. At the same time, it made it clear that ours is a planet like billions of others, and that our place in the scheme of things is, to say the least, not especially large.

An unobstructed gaze into the far distance has the value of returning us to a sense of proportion. I have often wondered whether the farmers of the American plains are better endowed with such a sense than we are in the cities. They live under a sky that an Englishman can only dream of. I don't know. It may be that familiarity breeds a boredom with the view, or that the economic plight of the American farmer presses more urgent matters to the fore of his mind. Certainly, to those of us less acquainted with it, an unobstructed view can shake the scales from our eyes. This was never more clear to me than when I went walking once in the Sahara. I had hired a guide to take me a day's camel ride out from the nearest town, and leave me on my own for three days. On my second day I walked way out on to the empty plain of the Ténéré, which stretched away in every direction as far as my eye could see. Not a rock or a dune marked the horizon, which merged in a shimmer with the sky. Walking in that land, without any of the usual bearings or landmarks, I had no sense of going in any particular direction. There was just the walking, rather than any idea of walking 'somewhere'. After an hour or so, I looked back to see how far I had come, and noticed that my footsteps were already being erased by the wind. My efforts and my sweat had left no trace at all on that empty world. In that instant, I felt unashamedly small, without even a story to tell. A burden I had not realized the weight of slipped from my shoulders, and I laughed to myself on the silent plain.

THE POWER OF THE IMAGE

Projection is a force to reckoned with; it is nothing less than the engine of life. Projection is what turns the world around; it literally keeps the action going. In India they respect and revere it as the force of *maya*. Maya does not mean illusion, or something non-existent, like a mirage. It means the constant flux of images and forms that are forever dissolving and arising through the gateways of birth and death.

All of us project images unceasingly, and through images we shape the world. They mobilize the human will and give us the structures within which to declare ourselves, to say and stand for what we believe in. Every thought we have ever had, even the most refined and elegant thoughts of all, are projections upon a reality that forever escapes definition. That does not mean they are false, but that they are working models which continually need to be revised according to the light of experience. An image turns sour when we insist on keeping it outside of the process of change; when we protect it from the new versions of reality that experience has subsequently revealed to us, or to the culture in general. Then a projection becomes a frozen image, a false god, and something in us becomes frozen as well, to the degree we are in its power.

A living image, however, can be seen to have a deeper reality than things or even people. St Thérèse of Lisieux is a case in point. During her life she was seen to be no one extraordinary, but through her writings and her actions, an image was created which exerted an extraordinary power after she died. For a long time, thousands of people were healed and converted to Christianity simply by visiting her shrine. The power was not in the girl who died young and more or less unknown, but in the image that was created by the intensity of her own faith and love. The image literally had the power to perform miracles.[6]

At a more common level, the image a person has of their doctor is as important an ingredient of their healing process as the medicine she prescribes. A major part of a healer's work is to create for the patient the image of a healer in whom they can trust and have confidence. Many people are alive today who would otherwise be dead just because they really believed an image. It was their image of the doctor that played the crucial part, not the doctor herself. If for any reason that image had been shattered, it would have been very much harder for the healing of the patient to take place.

In the same way, voters cast their vote for their perceived image of a politician, and not for the person who might be behind the role. The image is carefully constructed by a design and media team, and the politician has to learn the appropriate lines and expressions. When a real person steps out from behind the role and, for example, has an affair, he is seen not to comply with his public image and, in the English-speaking world, he is usually forced to resign. The politician rarely delivers on the promise of first impressions and yet it is a mark of the power of the image that we still go on voting for the same person or party long after we know their image is hollow. The Conservatives in Britain, for example, have developed throughout their history the image that they have a special flair and inside knowledge of economics. This has been an image which had become exceedingly hard to see through, whatever the reality of their performance. It is also true that we go along with old images not because they work, but out of habit; and because new ones have yet to emerge. The power to imagine is at the core of our humanity, and not always available to instant access. So in the personal and the collective sphere, we carry on as usual until some new image emerges to give us a fresh perspective and a new start. Habit, though, is a powerful taskmaster, and it takes courage to take our lives in our own hands and be willing to entertain new visions of ourselves and of the world. Courage or crisis, or a mixture of the two, can lead to creative action.

Whether we move or not, change or not, images govern our lives and our actions down to the tiniest detail. This is not always easy to accept, because the prevailing assumption about images is that they are somehow less than the reality. What is 'really there' is ourselves standing in front of a mirror. The image in the mirror is 'only an image', not really there at all. Yet if I am shaving, or brushing my hair, I have to concede that the image in the mirror is the source of my actions. It is only through following the image that I am carrying out the action.

Even in that simple situation, the image clearly has power over what I am doing. In the more complex areas of personal life, we follow images that are not of our conscious choosing, and that are largely out of our control. This is truer than ever when we fall in love. Then, the image of our beloved whirls us through the day as if we had been born into a new life. Their image is everywhere, on the edge of our every movement, bringing the most ordinary activities alive with new colour and meaning. Conventional wisdom says that love is blind. It is also true to say that lovers can see what most others can't. Even with its disappointments, its deceptions and failures, love holds an inexorable sway over the human soul. Even one look, as with Dante for Beatrice, can engender the inspiration and insight of a lifetime.[7]

Cynics and psychologists will murmur knowingly that lovers are infatuated with their own idealized parent, with their perfect hero, or the goddess of their dreams. They know that the euphoria will pass all too quickly, and the other aspects of the picture will eventually come to the fore – the witch, the jealous guardian, the angry father, the petulant child, and all the other figures we would prefer not to be three, but who recur with predictable regularity. Cynics know that most lovers today will end up in the divorce courts tomorrow.

All this can be true. We can literally be possessed by the magnet of love (or hate) to such a degree that we lose all sense of perspective. Yet this does not deny a further truth: the eyes of love do not entirely mislead. They see what is opaque to ordinary eyes. Their look reaches down into the eyes of the beloved and is held there by the passing back and forth of a current, a tangible sustenance for the innermost soul. In that look the whole body is brought alive. What lovers see in that gaze is none other than their own beauty, their own truth, revealed in the mirror of the other. Life takes on new meaning in love because love reveals us to ourselves precisely in the same moment that it reveals us to another. Love shows us the truth and freedom of our individuality at the very same time that it reflects our unity with another. Our troubles arise when we see only one half of the picture.

It is the same with projections of the negative kind. Projections bond us with another, for good or for ill. They are the manifest form of our unconscious needs intertwined with some external reality. The internal image and the external one either repel or fasten on to each other like a pair of magnets, holding both parties in a dance which is not of their choosing. We will be possessed by the projection to the degree that we remain unconscious of its origins – which are neither wholly within us, nor wholly without. The force of projection, though, seems to throw the onus for the situation entirely on to the other person, like a concealed film-projector throwing its image on to a screen. When we look daggers at someone, or with eyes of hate or loathing, we are convinced our disturbance is their doing alone. However, if we feel critical or judgemental in any degree, we can be sure of one thing: either we are envious of the person concerned for having a quality or circumstance that we feel we lack; or we are seeing in them something that we do not like in ourselves. We are all in some degree reflections of each other.

'What you see is what you are!' retorts my ten-year-old step-daughter when she is told off. Yes, but the truth is more complicated, for what we see is partly what the other is, too.

Where can the truth lie, then, in a world of so many reflections? Somewhere in the middle, perhaps, neither within nor without; in our willingness to keep looking for the larger view, even when we think we have got it; in the excitement of seeing the unfolding process, in the gasp of discovery when another layer peels away. Imagine what it would be like no longer to see with the eyes of blame; to exchange eyes that always needed to be in the right for eyes that were willing to explore.

It's all in a change of view. However, that is quite a change to make. Some views change quite gracefully in the light of evolving circumstances. There is a deeper view, however, that actually holds us. This is the view, the particular slant, of our soul. Our soul moulds our body, the way we walk, the way we reach for a glass on a table. We live in that view, we breathe it, even if we barely know it. We are made in our soul's image, the most enduring image of all. Though the conscious ego may seem to be little more than a compilation of parental and cultural views, that is only the tiniest portion of who we are. The soul is – we are – a deep well. That well is our responsibility, and it takes the form it does with our tacit approval. As long as we don't bother to look at it, it will do as it pleases with our lives. To look in the mirror can be a painful thing, as well as a pleasant surprise.

When we look, we shall see that the truth is more than we thought; and the more we look, the more the truth will grow. If we don't look, if we let the unconscious carry on living us as it wills, there will come a time when we will feel that our soul has slipped through our fingers. That is the time, though we won't know it, that the great goddess Maya will know she has won the day.

Icons and Idols

The purpose of an icon is to act as a doorway through to some deeper reality. The icon of a saint in an Orthodox Christian church exists to lead the believer, through the contemplation of its form, beyond that form to an experience of the presence of the saint himself and of the whole communion of saints; and even beyond that, to a realm in which all images have faded away. An image of this kind is a living symbol of the invisible world it points to. It acts as a focus for the believer's devotion, and channels its intensity through the world of form to another, discernible only to an inner eye.

In the secular world, a Turner landscape, a Vermeer interior, a Rembrandt portrait, can lead us beyond the predictable confines of the temporal into a surprising, deeper, and more substantial relationship with ourselves and the world. Art of this quality can generate feelings of awe, wonder, delight, a sense of the numinous, an uncanny sense of recognition. In the presence of great art we are never diminished; not made to feel less, but more, than we usually experience ourselves to be. We can be taken beyond ourselves, and returned to ourselves with interest.

In this way, art can serve as an icon. Sacred images arise from the notion of the incarnation of a cosmic individual who has come to redeem the world, be he Christ, Krishna, or a Bodhisattva. For the believer, the icon is a bridge that can connect him to the living reality of the Redeemer. That reality can be revealed through the doorway of the icon because it exists not only in the fabric of the universe, but also within ourselves. The icon, through the imagination, serves to join the inner and the outer and reveal to us our infinite nature.

Art can do this too. Today, anything at all that consolidates our deepest sense of truth and goodness into an image can serve a similar function. A simple photograph of a woman,[8] someone she has never met, has served as an icon for someone I know, more than any work of art or religious object. It is not a specific kind of image that makes something an icon, so much as the quality of the looking that it evokes from the viewer. A Rembrandt, or even a Russian icon, is no longer sacred in most people's eyes just because of its origins. The holy images of the Catholic Church were seen by the Puritans of the seventeenth century as graven images, and they pulled many of them down. Iconoclasm has erupted periodically throughout the history of Christian-

ity. It is not so simple today to make literal distinctions between what is sacred and what is not. With the liberalization
and questioning of belief systems, and a growing awareness
of the many different forms in which the human spirit ex-
presses itself around the globe, we find it more natural to respect that what might have no meaning for us may well be
an icon for somebody else.

What ultimately distinguishes the idol from the icon is
the presence or absence of imagination. If an image evokes
the imagination, it can draw a person toward the deeper
reality of their own existence. An image of this kind is endless: it can take a person as far into themselves as they are
willing to go. As soon as it is seen literally, however – at its
surface level alone – it loses it power and falls to the status of
an idol. A Rembrandt becomes an idol when it is valued for
its signature alone, or for its current price in the art market.
On the one hand the Puritans were blind to the symbolic
reality of the images they tore down, seeing them as mere
sculptures of stone; on the other, it was true that the Church
had lost its own sensitivity to the deeper significance of its
images. Without that sensitivity, its images were indeed no
more than idols. What the Puritans did, like so many icono-
clasts before them, was to fight blindness with blindness.

Our contemporary idols shine out at us from every
glossy magazine, from advertising hoardings in the street,
on T-shirts, posters, and in the corner of our living room,
from out of the little black box. In this era of the image, the

whole world is their temple; they are everywhere, always in our mind's eye, whether we want them or not. Schwarzenegger, Madonna, Michael Jackson, the Royal Family, the cast of Dallas, the latest faces of fashion, there are enough of them for everyone to have their own favourite.

In March 1992 I bought a copy of *Cosmopolitan* magazine. It was the magazine's twentieth anniversary. The first few pages showed a cover girl from every year since the magazine was started, twenty beautiful women, each one inviting me to feast my eyes on her. It was an incredible sight. Yet what struck me more than their seductive looks was that every face had a gloss, a manufactured smile or pout for the camera. A single match had more warmth than all of them put together. Every one of those faces was a frozen beauty. Like any idol, they were a manufactured image, and nothing but the image. Their faces were opaque, two-dimensional masks, with no one behind them. After the initial dazzle of opening the page, I couldn't help feeling they looked a sorry sight – the sacrificial lambs of the image-makers whose job it is to sell a concept – a publishing concept, a fashion concept, a 'look' that can sell hair-styler, lipstick, glamour and sex, a whole way of life.

What do we see in our idols that makes us continue to sustain them with our purchasing power? For one thing, they give an easy solution to our desire to spend. The fabrication of attractive images makes it easier to decide on which record, movie seat, dress or coat to buy. We buy the packaging, not the product. But what makes their image attractive? A certain seduction, a knowing look, the image of fame, wealth and glamour. Above all, we want what we actually give them: success. They bask in it, and reflect it back to us, which seduces us even more. We keep on buying, and they keep coming up with the goods. As long as we remain content with second-hand experience rather than tasting the real thing, our fantasies and appetites will be inexhaustible, and we shall never be able to see beyond them. The real thing is the light of our own, first-hand experience; our own radiance, which will always be more substantial and satisfying than somebody else's charisma. No idol can ever give us that. When an image does not draw us beyond itself, it becomes a vacuum, a shadow play, inherently empty. An empty thing cannot make us full. We go on buying more and more shadows in the inarticulate hope that one of them will hit the mark. If in doubt, go shopping.

Our own radiance eventually emerges in the light of its recognition. That is what we really want, if the truth be known. Recognition of our talents, of our value in the community; but more, much more than that: secretly, we feel there is something in us that is larger, more expansive than the person we normally experience ourselves to be. And there is. There is – beneath the veneer of our cool and reasonable world – an abundance which hides in our veins. A faint memory of it lives in our consciousness still, and we want it. We know, at some level beneath our words, that without the expression of that simple joy, the affirmation of being alive, we are not being fully seen for who we are. We may like to fantasize that buying 'the look' will get us the recognition we want. But it doesn't. So we pay our dues to Madonna, or somebody else, to do it for us instead.

All they can give us, however, is our own recycled fantasies, which turn around on themselves with a pleasure that can only be private and solitary, mind masturbations. You can't have a relationship with an idol; neither, through the medium of an idol, can you have much of a relationship with yourself. An idol, then, is thoroughly anti-sensuous. For all its apparent sex and glamour, it only titillates our surface sensations. An icon is an icon precisely because it draws us into relationship with the deepest levels of life. It is full of soul, then; bursting with sensuousness. An idol survives only as long as we fail to recognize the value and joy in ourselves. An icon, however ordinary or humble it may be, can lead us straight to that deeper recognition.

CHIMNEY POTS

My bedroom is four stories up, and out of my window a streetful of chimneypots marches down the hill as if they were defending in ranks the green hills behind them. Three rows, with forty pots between them, sit right there before me in the very place I first saw them six years ago. Only a TV aerial has joined the original crowd, pinned like an outrider on to the edge of the first row.

The middle row has a king in the middle with four queens, two either side, and a company of solemn sentinels forming the flanks. A king pot has a crown. This one is six-pointed, with a fine double rim, and another rim near the base, just where it begins to flange out into the stack. Now, I am not making this up: there are king pots, there are queen pots, and there are pots. I know this because last year we had a new chimney stack built. Mr Calder, the chimneypot man, asked us what kind of pot we wanted. 'Kings and queens are antiques, now,' he said. 'An expensive business. I'd go for a more modern one, myself.' So we did.

The crown of the pack I can see from my window is a fine pot, an old pot, perhaps a hundred years old, the colour of ochre; like the walls of the patrician buildings that line the main square in Siena. A clay pot, an ochre clay king pot with four queens almost the same colour but not quite, with crowns slightly smaller than their lord's; and leaning ever so slightly towards him with a barely disguised affection. He, though, is straight, careful not to bestow his attentions on one side any more than the other. That, I imagine, is what in any event king pots might be expected to do. Stand straight. Or at least, during the day. At night, it may be a different matter. I have never seen the chimneypots at night. I can't, and they probably know that.

The queens have six points on their crowns, too; sharp

points, finely chiselled; not quite so high as the king's, but just as pretty, each one with an angle all of its own which measures the field behind into uneven pieces. Two of the queens have more colour in their bodies than the others, almost a pink flush. They all look as old as the king, though with chimneypots, the older you are, the more beautiful you look, and the higher your price.

Their companion sentinels are younger, and taller by a rim, perhaps two feet tall, even though they have no crowns. They end in a lip which is folded back and down for perhaps two centimetres. From the lip they descend in straight lines faintly diverging to end in the stack. They are a simple statement of a chimneypot. I am sure they do the job, though I wouldn't know, because chimneypots are usually on night shift. I am simply going by their statement, which seems honest enough. The truth is, they are dull pots. They are a dull red, with black stains crawling all over them. They have no relations in Siena. They probably came from Birmingham, or Workington, or Barry, which is over the river in Wales. I am sure they do the job, though.

I have not wanted to think this thought, but I suppose I must tell the whole truth: I don't really think it's the night work that stops me seeing their puffing and blowing. I think the king, the queens, the young ones, all of them are redundant. I don't think any of them have worked in years. And the reason I think this is that next to the last queen on the left is a nasty little aluminium spout that pokes out of the stack by just a few inches. To be accurate, then, the three stacks carry forty pots, a television aerial, and the other protrusion. I didn't want to mention it when I started out. It's not a pot. But I have to admit that I have often seen it smoking. No, I have seen it steaming. It doesn't smoke, it steams. Central heating steam, boiler steam, hot-water steam. One, or all, of those, I suppose. One ugly little spout has knocked the steam out of all those pots.

It will never steal their crowns, though; nor their delight to the eyes. It will never be more than a squat little round thing choking every now and then on a head of steam. Mr Calder, the chimneypot man, told us what he could. But if we ever put another pot up there on our own stack, I shall make it a king pot, or a queen; even though, once it was up there, we would never see it again. Then someone else, further up the hill, could look out of their window and see the royalty I see now.

A Collection of Looks on the Way to the Post Office

an old man with a preoccupied look

a fat man in grey staring bleakly ahead

a smile of recognition

a look and a look away with a woman in blue

a young girl looking ahead

a glazed, rolling eye from a drunk sprawled on the steps of the
NatWest Bank

the laughing eyes of a girl stepping over him

Look! Our prices are down!

the eyes of a saint rolled up to heaven in a picture in the antique
shop

an affectionate look from a mother to her little boy

the brown bead eyes of a wooden pig staring blankly out of the
butcher's window

a long look at two long legs in black tights

two women, then a man in a grey overcoat, almost invisible, but I
see them

the postmistress has a cold, and she looks up at me with streaming
eyes

Making Eyes

Sexuality is everywhere, in the office, the street, the department store, and in the old people's homes as well as the schools. But more than anywhere else, sexuality is in the eyes. A look can lead to a word, a word can progress to a touch, and on to the intimacies of taste and smell. Of all the millions of looks that take place in a single high street, only a very few of them ever lead to their ultimate conclusion. Not many even form into a word or a smile. The majority of them – the furtive glance, the sidelong look, the glimpse out of the corner of an eye – evaporate without leaving a trace. Many, on the other hand, are picked up and noticed. For a moment, two people may register that the other exists, and that the recognition is mutual.

It is in those milliseconds of recognition that the desire to make contact may arise – not a personal contact, to begin with anyway, but a contact of energy, an exchange, a play of looks. Enter the time-honoured ritual of flirtation. The back and forth of the tiniest variations of gesture, glance, and posture, a language so fast and fine of detail, so prehistoric in its origins, that both parties are caught up in a play they only partly understand; a play that entirely defies the rationality of contemporary political correctness.

Flirtation arises from deep in our instinctive brains; from the same region that drives peacocks to fan their tails, and cats to bristle their fur. Unlike the peacocks, however, we have the blessing-curse of self-consciousness; as soon as our instinctive reactions emerge, we become conscious of them, and our self-image comes into play. The game of conquest is then transferred from the strictly physical sphere to the psychic one – the eyes may be giving appreciation and recognition, and seeking the same in return.

Flirtation for the sake of it is a play without resolution, suspended in a passing moment that neither party dares or even wants to bring to ground. That is its attraction. The flirting eye moves quickly from instinctive reaction to fantasy, playing with the possible, and fed by the partly or suggestively revealed. It can be fun. It can be downright lascivious. A man will often undress a woman in the street with his eyes, at times hardly even knowing he is doing it. Perhaps it happens the other way round as well, though I am not aware of having had the experience. Women I have asked about this say their reactions to it will vary. Often they will feel invaded; they will feel taken advantage of. At other times they will feel aroused by it, or flattered. It remains true that a woman usually grooms herself to be looked at. The man looks. He may seem to be in control, yet often, like the flower with the bee, she has taken the original initiative, and she can discard his look with the turn of a cheek and deflate his chest like a collapsed balloon. It takes two to dance; if a flirtatious look is rejected, it will usually be replaced with embarrassment.

I usually find myself giving women looks that are not so much flirtatious, in the sense that I want some relationship with them, transitory or otherwise, but appreciative. I enjoy the form of woman, the figure she cuts, the beauty of her line, her head of hair, the way she moves. I enjoy the light that sometimes flits around her edges. And at times, all of this, I readily admit, can have more than a tinge of lust. I am happy, though, to look without reciprocation. The trouble is, it is not easy to steal a look. People know when someone is looking, even in the space of a second.

It happened yesterday, in the station. As I walked in my eyes went of their own volition to a very long, thin woman in tight trousers and jaunty short jacket who was pushing a child backwards and forwards in his pushchair. I had hardly registered that my eyes were on her, when I realized she was returning my gaze. 'Hey, jerk, what do you want?' her eyes said. I hadn't realized I wanted anything, though perhaps I did. I just thought I was meeting someone off a train. Her wide, pouting mouth and dark red lips, high cheekbones with wisps of black hair, her lean frame squeezed into a mean set of clothes (how did I register all that in less than a second?), everything about her said, 'You don't mess with me'. But I meant no harm: my eyes preceded me, just looking, on my way to meet a friend from a train. I wasn't there to make eyes or spar with her. Since I was waiting, though, and the train was late, I looked again as if I was looking at the timetable display behind her head. Her jaw jutted out and she looked with a pout straight in my eye. I looked away at the timetable display. I stood there, knowing there was nothing in me that intended any wrong, nor even any particular attraction; knowing, too, that I was not entirely innocent either. All in the space of three seconds.

It's another matter when a look breaks out into a smile, or a word. Then, what is happening is out in the open. There is a certain tension that accompanies the subliminal world of instinctual exchange, the unconscious swapping of looks. A stolen look, or a flirtatious gaze that is unacknowledged as such, can be a separating, an isolating thing. The trouble with either is that it can treat the other person as an object, there simply for the gratification or the fuelling of our own fantasies. A smile or a word makes a bridge; it recognizes the other as a person in their own right, as well as the stimulus of our desire. Just making contact, person to person, dissolves the posturing and its tension. What a relief, when the reciprocal snatching of sidelong glances is broken with a genuine smile. A smile that recognizes and appreciates the value of another human being.

There is something else that can break the spell. Sometimes I am quick enough to notice my gaze being magnetized by a woman in the street, and instead of letting my attention travel along its beam, I fall in with the breath in my belly. Rising and falling, rising and falling. That brings me into my body, and off the hook of the passing attraction. A wonderful, though simple, thing happens then. I see the woman not as a desirable object, from which I am separate; but as a person with her own value walking her way in the world of the street. If an instant before my gaze was keeping her at a distance, now, without even looking at her, I can feel the warmth of our common lot. She is still attractive, and I still enjoy the fact; but I am no longer a prisoner of my own gaze. If our eyes do meet, and I am following the course of my breath, the looking can take its course without the normal self-consciousness, the power play, or any of the other obstructions to simple seeing.

Sometimes, the eyes will carry us down into a relationship of forces deeper than our conscious mind and lighter, freer, than the knee-jerk reactions of the genitals. We are just sitting there on the tube train and suddenly we are looking straight into the soul of the person opposite, a complete stranger, while they, at the same time, are gazing down into ours. For no reason, who knows why, there we are brimming with life, suddenly so full we could laugh out loud. We feel warm, ample, defenceless, without deceit. Who needs to avert a gaze that streams like a river and that goes to feed an ocean inside us we have heard of, but never named? At the next stop they get up and leave, and we never see them again. What has passed between us in those few moments is the quintessence of humanity.

Such a meeting could be the start of falling in love. On the other hand, it may not necessarily be any such thing. If we fall in love with everyone we open our hearts to, we may find ourselves in an awkward predicament. Love is more than the sharing of hearts; it is a stronger medicine still. It does strange things to a person's eyes. They will keep seeing the image of their beloved even when they are absent. 'The seizure that comes from the meeting of the eyes', as the troubadours used to describe it in the Middle Ages. The troubadours, the singer-poets of the twelfth century, were the first to conceive of romantic love as we do today. Even though arranged marriages – decided between the respective families for their general benefit – continued to be the norm for centuries afterwards, the ideal of personal, romantic love that the troubadours initiated became a distinctive characteristic of Western culture from the twelfth century onwards. Joseph Campbell, the American mythologist, took up the troubadour's language and style when he said,

> So through the eyes love attains the heart, for the eyes are the scouts of the heart. . . . And when they are in full accord and firm, all three, in one resolve, at that time perfect love is born from what the eyes have made welcome to the heart. For as all true lovers know, love is perfect kindness, which is born, there is no doubt, from the heart and the eyes.[9]

Yet when two lovers are together, I have known lightning to crackle between them. The look of love can also be a dangerous thing. It reveals all that we are, and all that we can be. Once, when my eyes met those of a woman I loved, there was such an electricity passing between us that I felt I was being burnt to a cinder. My whole body trembled, and I had to turn away to feel I would survive. Now, nearly twenty years later, it sounds like I am exaggerating for effect. The shudder of that gaze, though, left me with a permanent mark, and I shall never forget the woman who shared it.

The Look in Their Eyes

I wonder how many people can remember the look in the eyes of their mother when they were young. That loving look, or the lack of it, can seal people's fates for the rest of their lives. It can give us the certainty that we have the right to exist, it can make us feel inherently recognized; or it can abandon us to the experience of a meaningless world in which we feel profoundly unloved.[10] The mother's look can be our first blessing or our first curse; for most of us, it is a mixture of the two. It can be the root of our security, through which we know we are loved; or it can be the source of a persistent sense of unworthiness which drives us to seek elsewhere the recognition we did not receive. In this latter case, the esteem of others will become the litmus of our own inherent sense of value, and any rejection or disregard will tend to lead to depression and self-loathing. The mother's look that helps us to stand on our feet is one of positive regard; a look that recognizes and responds to our essential personhood, and that makes us feel at home in ourselves. It is the look of unconditional love. It can take a moment, and last a lifetime. One reason that the mother's look can have such an effect is that the infant's eyes are wide open, unfiltered as yet to the immensity pouring in on them daily. They are eyes of wonder, astonishment, fear, sadness, all the great emotions pass over them with little obstruction, in response to the world around.

A second blessing we may be fortunate to receive is the look of the father. This is likely to come in our later childhood, or our teens, if it comes at all. It is the look of interest and approval, which tells us we are worth listening to. It is a look that brings us into the world and confirms that we have a rightful place in the community. It is a complement to the mother's look, that made us feel at home in ourselves. The father's blessing is compounded when we are noticed by our elders in our chosen work or profession. The affirming look of the father, and of teachers and older role models, is a look that takes us seriously. It is a look that coaxes us to believe in ourselves. We can see and feel their interest in us, which galvanizes our own interest and spurs us to make efforts and undertake discipline.

There is a look we can give each other as adults that can help heal some of the gap we may have felt in our childhood. A person's bearing, and especially their eyes, shows their sadness, their hope, their struggle, their defeat, their brightness, their knowing, their substance or lack of soul. We can all be read like a book, though we might ask with good reason what right anyone has to read in such a way those texts that a person might prefer to keep private. Everything depends on the manner of looking. There is prying, staring, observing, watching, all of them in different degrees an imposition from a detached perspective. There is another way of looking which does not separate, but joins with another in empathy. This kind of looking does not take away anything from a person, it adds something to them: the warmth of human compassion and understanding.

We do not need to be a counsellor or a doctor to hold someone in such a regard; we simply need to be human. What I am referring to is a manner of looking that can best be described by the old-fashioned word 'beholding'. If we behold a person, there is a softness in our eyes, rather than the searchlight that is switched on with a stare. If we behold someone, we are not trying to do anything with them; we are not even trying to be helpful, or understanding. We are not taking any posture at all. Beholding is a wholly receptive activity, and when we behold someone we are simply with them, even if they don't know we are there. Rather than this or that attribute or defect, we will see another person's heart beating, no different to our own. Not only our eyes, but our whole body, our whole person, will be with them.

We can do almost anything with our eyes: eyes can seduce, they can undress, they can reduce us to a shrivel, they can charm, enchant, deceive and hypnotize. They can look through us, pierce us with arrows; and looks can even kill. Belief in the evil eye holds strong still in most parts of Africa and the Middle East. If a person of power, a practitioner of shamanism or witchcraft, shines the look of death on some unfortunate, then that person's belief system will ensure that they waste away.

The eyes have traditionally been used to transmit spiritual power from master to disciple in religious traditions all over the world. Irene Tweedie,[11] a Russian émigrée in her eighties living in London, told me a remarkable story about spiritual transmission. She is herself a teacher of the Sufi path of spiritual practice. One night, some years ago, she had a vivid dream that took place in Morocco. She saw a village with pink houses that was somewhere on the way to Marrakech, and even though she did not know the place, she knew there was a monastery there she was meant to visit. That same week she flew to Morocco, and took the bus from Tangier to Marrakech. As they were passing through a village on the way, she recognized the place in her dream. She got out of the bus and asked a boy nearby to direct her to the local spiritual community. He took her to the *tekke*, as it was called, on the hill behind the village. It was a compound with a few small buildings encircled by a high wall. As she came in the gate in the wall she saw the head of the monastery in front of her. A few disciples were sitting at his feet. He gazed at her with a long, steady look that stopped her in her tracks. Then he looked away. She knew that that look was what she had come for, and without a word she turned and left, and came immediately back to London.

$\mathcal{T}$HE $\mathcal{P}$HOTOGRAPHIC $\mathcal{E}$YE

Through a telephoto lens, the daisies round a tree in the street stand out suddenly with unusual clarity, each petal worthy of a picture. I had not even noticed them before. The ragged edge of a billboard cuts a visually interesting line across the viewfinder, and as some passer-by stands unknowingly for a moment in the sights of my shutter, I catch sight of the texture of the blue cloth of his jacket and the seams of his pocket. The camera directs the eye to where it would normally never go, to the particular, the detail, the unusual juxtaposition or angle; to a composition which, without the selectivity of the camera's eye, would merge into the broad and humdrum flux of life.

The camera has become the primary democratic means for displaying an individual point of view. It is the instrument which, above all others, encourages and facilitates a heightened visual sensibility. 'In my view,' said Émile Zola in 1901, after several years of amateur photography, 'you cannot really say you have seen something until you have photographed it.'[12] The camera has not only increased our capacity to see what we normally wouldn't, with high technology macro lenses, and all the rest; it has fundamentally changed our way of seeing itself. It has elevated to the state of art the activity of seeing for seeing's sake. Weston, the great American photographer of the 1930s, said that the point of his work was to show people what their own un-seeing eyes had missed.

Anything, through a lens, can take on an unusual presence. Almost anything can seem beautiful, and everything can certainly be interesting. Beauty, once confined to highly limited subjects and arrangements, has been democratized through the camera to include ususual shots of trash cans; close-ups of cigarette ends; the back walls and fire-escapes of tenement buildings; any part of the human body or the natural world; red tiles on a Provençal roof; windows, doors, and old fireplaces. The camera leaves no stone unturned in its pursuit of unsuspected charm or interest. More than anything else, it can find the remarkable in the ordinary. Everything and anything, from the right angle, can be transformed from a fleeting impression into an immortal event. That event, like Doisneau's shot of the couple kissing in a Paris street, can then be sold in print shops in all the capitals of the world.

I took to using my camera again a couple of years ago, after a lapse of some twenty years. But now, after several photographic journeys, some of my old concerns about the photographic eye – which caused me to set it aside for so long – are demanding consideration again. My own intent in picking up my camera again had something to do with a belief expressed by Ansel Adams. He proclaimed that one should not set out to 'take' a photograph, so much as to 'make' it; and that the camera was an instrument of love and revelation.[13] I would like to think that many of my photographs have been 'made', rather than 'taken'. They are constructions, following the inner aesthetic of the eye, usually of landscapes. When people enter the picture, I find it hard not to admit that, however constructed in the sense above, it also requires a 'taking' – something is covertly stolen from the persons concerned – a posture, a movement, an expression – that they were not even aware of having, and that I appropriated for my own satisfaction. I can't help feeling that in that instant my photographic gaze, however much it appreciated their grace or beauty, diminished them in some way to the status of an object, there for the having.

The presence of the element of having obscures the capacity for a photograph to be loving, to celebrate the subject rather than to capture it. Photographs – all photographs – tend by nature to be acquisitive. In having, possession, not love, is the dominant tone; in using, power, not love, is the primary motivation. Neither of these forms of relationship, having and using, go far beyond treating the world as an object. As long as we see others and the world as objects, we perpetuate our sense of separation from life. We entrench ourselves in the observer position and evade the intimate sense of unity among equals we so often seem to be seeking. In taking up the camera again, I immediately became aware and wary of its dual nature: it brings me close to the world through the intense appreciation it fosters of life's unending interest and beauty; and at the same time, the easy option is to allow it to keep me apart from life, in the safe position of an observer who can never enter into engaged relationship with what he is observing.

Even so, like many other photographers, I have felt that the camera has afforded me a genuine intimacy at times with a landscape or an object. Such photographs were taken in a mood of contemplation, or quiet reflection; and in that mood, the land I was in opened itself more willingly to my eyes. I, in my turn, was open to it, letting it mould me as I was moulding it through my camera. There is no doubt that I have been shaped thus in some way by the desert, by Provence, and by India.

Something else comes into play, however, when I show people my slides. The photographs are no longer reflections of moments in the desert, they are a reality in their own right. An appreciation or criticism of them is not an evaluation of their subject, but of the photograph, in and as itself. Photography has superimposed on the concrete world another one, no less real – the world of images. A photograph is a stencil of the real. It is the registration of emanations, light waves, reflected by objects. It is an actual material vestige of something or someone, an extension of them which can survive their death and still have an aura of its own.

Once taken, the photograph assumes its own independent reality. The image world is more real, and has more power, in contemporary culture, than the concrete world of living beings. It is not uncommon for people to feel more real when they see their photograph. They can seem even more real if they manage to get on television, because, more than anything else, an image acknowledges the presence, the there-ness, of its subject, and that presence is confirmed by the witness of millions of viewers. To have one's image in hand may seem like an easy route to self-affirmation. That it isn't, is fairly obvious; yet to disregard the power of the image is not to see what is before our eyes: our world is run by images. Much of our personal life, the life of our desires, is determined by them.

For primitive people the photograph is a magical tool which can have power over its subject. It has frozen a moment in their time and lifted it out of its context into another reality, the world of images. From there, they can be reached, wherever they are. I am wary of this magical dimension of photography because I sense it to have far deeper implications than our present awareness is willing to credit it with. We do take something in a photograph which is more than the material emanation of light; not only from people but also from things and from nature. We take, usually without giving back. Photography is, above all else, the art of consumerism.

At the same time, images have an éclat which can startle us into life and action, they can galvanize the will, open the eyes to beauty, give us information that would otherwise be out of our reach, and nudge the conscience of a whole nation into action (as in the case of the press photo of the Vietnamese girl alight with napalm running down a street). Images have great power that is satisfying to both producer and consumer. The problem is that their hold on the attention is diminished in proportion to their exposure. Suffering, for example, is already over-exposed, and people turn away from yet more images of starving Africa. The beauty of lavender in a field, of a sunset, of ocean rollers, becomes a cliché through over-exposure.

Photographs of suffering and of beauty can perpetuate the distance between observer and observed, while giving a simultaneous sensation of intimacy. The intimacy created is nearly always sentimental, because it is based on an idea – an image – and not on the concrete experience. An artist in the traditional sense – writer, painter, sculptor, musician – draws the suffering and the beauty of the world into himself and transmutes it through his own lived experience into a work of art. He is an alchemical retort who can himself be changed in some subtle manner by the creative process that is fermenting within him. The suffering and beauty of the world become part of his own physical, as well as mental, experience. This is not what always, or even often, happens in art. But it can, and does, happen. Artists can make/create themselves through their work. It is less easy for a photographer to do this because the whole process happens outside of him. Life is observed, and instead of being absorbed and distilled into his own flesh, it can more easily pass him by.

For someone who wants to engage with life, rather than be a tourist through it, photography is a questionable, if attractive art. The imagination, eye of the soul, is given substance less by images, however stirring, than by the steep side of a solid mountain, by rushing rivers, by fallen trees that block one's path, and by all manner of first-hand engagements with the world. The derivative world of images is as likely to diminish our capacity for seeing as it is to intensify it. That is why I am trying now to take photographs sparingly, rather than mindlessly adding to the vast heaps of surfeit images our culture is wading through already.

Seeing the Whole in the Part

I was sitting in a wood one day when my eyes fell on a beech tree in front of me. For a moment there was a gap in the train of my thoughts, and instead of having another thought about the beech tree – without even thinking 'beech tree' at all – I *saw* this creature insinuating itself into the air, thrusting its way upwards like an arm out of the ground. I could feel the life of this thing in my body. It was a living power which filled a portion of space and met me, faced me fair and square with the fact of itself. I could think about the fact afterwards, but right there and then its existence, as solid and as substantial as my own, demanded all my attention and would have no truck with reflections. I could not avoid the power of its life pouring into an upward motion.

The strange thing was that when my eyes fell on the grass at the base of the tree, there was the same power, in a different, but no less potent form. The teeming life of a million blades showering out of the ground. When I caught sight of that life in the tree and the grass, it registered as a sensation of awe. Awe is a recognition of power, even majesty. Occasionally, an individual will bespeak awe; their life shines through the container of their social face. More often, it is some grand stroke of Nature that awakens the sensation, like a mighty waterfall, thunder and lightning, or the rolling ocean. Awe makes our hair stand on end. A step in another direction, and it would be fear; except awe urges us not to fight or flee, but to stand and stare. I had never known awe at the sight of grass before; but what made my hair bristle on the back of my neck was not the particular form of the grass or the tree; it was the undifferentiated power of life that was pouring through them. It was not so much that I could see this power, but that I could sense it as a bodily experience; it impressed itself upon my imagination not as a sight but as something I was breathing in.

After a few minutes, or seconds, I don't know how long, I began to see the trunk and branches of the particular tree, different to every other tree in the wood. As the vision of its living power receded, its particular shape and history began to take up my mind. I could see now how it had had to bend to the left to steal some light from its neighbours; how it had had a branch lopped off in some winter storm, and how its particular place in the forest had helped determine its shape, its direction, its colouration, and size. A moment before, I had been filled with awe; now, the particular personality of this tree was inviting what I can only describe as a sense of intimate kinship, almost a kind of love. This tree was an individual now, with its own voice.

A few minutes more, and its individuality began to merge with what I already knew about trees, with memories, stories, and associations. I began daydreaming again: of the dark and dangerous places in fairy stories, of owls hooting and foxes running, the cracking of twigs in the silent night. I wondered how old this wood was, and whether it was recognized as a part of our natural heritage; who managed it, who owned it; and whether there was anything we could do to help preserve the rainforest. What was before me in the shape of a particular tree had merged back into the wood.

Back in the familiar realm of reflection, I was aware how easily I usually satisfied myself with assumed knowledge and experience; how, usually, I allow what I see only to corroborate what I already know, so that it was rare that I saw anything new. Most of us, I suppose, rarely see anything other than our own explanations. Our store of words and images recycles itself endlessly, and acts as a veil – a necessary one, perhaps – between ourselves and a deeper reality.

Nature is obscured not only by our existing concepts, but also by our manufactured emotions – by sentimentality. We imagine we are meant to feel certain feelings in Nature. We have learnt that it is beautiful, peaceful, restoring, and good for us. We have almost entirely removed ourselves from the experience of those who live and work in Nature – foresters, shepherds, fishermen – who know that She is a force to be reckoned with. Nature is often dark, and dangerous, and always worthy of respect. We have put technology between ourselves and the elements, and we nurture the illusion that the earth is at our mercy, and not the other way around. Nature will do as we command, and we shall view her charms from the marked footpaths and the car window. From a seemingly safe vantage point, we run the danger of trying to feel what we are meant to feel; in the process, we separate ourselves not only from the woods, but also from ourselves. This is sentimentality, and it always rings hollow.

In its currently fashionable form, sentimentality commonly emerges as a desire to bestow our wish for spiritual feelings on the trees, or the land. This particular place is a power spot, we murmur in hushed tones. Feel the energy with your hands. The Celts considered this a holy place. Or we talk to the trees, we hug them, or call them brother. Go through the motions, popular pschology has it, and you will get the genuine feeling. Maybe. The body is certainly connected to the feeling life in a way the mind can never be. But then it must be the body that leads, and not the mind. If the mind tells us it is good to hug a tree, the mind will manufacture the appropriate feeling. If the body reaches out for no reason and embraces an oak, we might feel the life in a real tree, instead of completing the self-fulfilling prophecy of our own image of what hugging a tree is like. Then, with the body mindlessly reaching out for the tree, we also have the freedom of not having to feel anything in particular at all. Just a hug of a tree, and that's that.

If the mind prompts us to move, we are likely to get neither the simple feeling of something, nor the simple reaction of nothing. More probably, we shall end up with a complex amalgam of something and nothing. A hollow something. That is not imagination. It is fantasy and daydream, and it is how we lose much of our own power and vision.

It's not easy, but we can only see the deeper layers of Nature with what I would call an empty eye. An eye that, for a moment or two, has slipped through its own images and preconceptions, and can see what is there. It's not easy, but the main thing is that we don't try. As soon as we try, we take the lid off the store of our existing images, or we begin to drum up the appropriate feelings. There is even no need to try and stop our own images. They have their own life, and we can let them run their own course. There is a soft, focused attention, not part of the thinking mind, that is sensitive to life even as our thoughts do what they do. To let that attention come more to the foreground, it is better to let ourselves be taken for a walk, so to speak; and instead of contemplating a river or a wood in order to have this or that insight or feeling, to let ourselves be with it for its own sake, without wishing for any particular outcome, simply sensitive to what is around us.

When we don't ask, we might receive. Or we might not. If the eye is empty for a moment, we might feel the feelings we have tried so hard at other times to feel. But that won't happen if you or I are merely content with these words. These words are several stages down the line from what was once a moment of seeing. One moment of real experience can generate a bookful of words. To see into the heartland, better to go for a walk on the wild side of the woods.

 STILL LIFE?

In my living room, by the window, is a large, round table with a large blue bowl on it, rounder still. A pewter hotplate, another round thing, reflects its face in the wide, ample body of the big blue bowl. That blue bowl fills me with satisfaction, I don't know why. It's a thick blue bowl, a peasant of a bowl, with a fat lip running right round its rim. It possesses a few grubby fingermarks, a scattering of dust, and some long, silver slivers of light from the window. Its blue is the rich blue of a Persian carpet; not a dark blue, a luminous blue which warms my face like the brush of velvet. It asks me to hold out my hands to its welcoming lip; and I do, surprised by the cool touch of china.

Today, a doddery leek leans against the inside of the rim, supported on the one side by a wrinkled Cox apple and a bright yellow lemon. Neatly interposed between the leek and the apple is the small reflection, perfectly proportioned, of the window on the other side of the room. The people walking by outside the house are captured for an instant in the inside of my bowl as their shadows flit past that window. To be held between an apple and a leek in a fruitbowl and never to know it.

The fate of the leek seems sealed. I wonder if he knows what I do, his own decay and dissolution already into the twilight hour. I wonder who knows what I do not, looking at me as I look at the leek. This is not a sorry leek, though, simply a leek turning yellow, its curling top with patches of earth still clinging to its inner sheaths bared now by the collapse of its outer shell. That outer shell is white now, with only a wisp of its former green, and even that fading to yellow; every vein and nerve in its body revealed unashamedly to anyone's eye. To anyone who cares to look. I care. I have never known such beauty as this fading leek, melting before my eyes like wax in a summer sun. Its last breath is passing without a hint of resistance. The last ripening, the relief and pleasure of taking off the tight shoe of a leek skin. Without taking the time to look, I would never have known that death could be as sensuous as this; and all of it unfolding so lightly.

The apple that props up the languid leek is a crusty old thing. He lends his outward belly curve to his failing companion not through some inherent compassion of fruit to veg, but in sullen resignation to the necessity brought about by proximity. He bears it without grinning. I have never noticed before the relation between a wrinkled apple and a fat old frog. But there it is for the eye to see: a frog in the apple, squatting there with distended belly and wrinkles all round his eye. It is a small apple, but a full one, full to bursting. With what? With soft white flesh and streaming juices, though you would never know from the wrinkles.

The lemon, however, is a bright yellow lemon, an unblemished yellow all the way round, that catches the light of even a winter sun. It too is full, tightly full; but it does not draw my juices as the apple does. No, it jolts me awake with its sunny splash, but it keeps me at a bowl's distance with a foreknowledge of its bitter interior. It cares nothing, of course, for my predilections. It will go on being a bright yellow lemon whatever I say; a brilliant shout from the Mediterranean, essence of southern fruit alone in a blue bowl with remote northern relations. Alone, but not lonely; a stout lemon, it is, proud of its origins, trailing figs and grapes through the eye of my mind. Like all things, this lemon lives an unfathomed life. It waits in the shadows of our unconcern to be revealed in a moment's attention. I know I have not seen it yet. It knows, too; though it knows how to wait. It is I who wonder about the time.

OLOURS

Oh, what in you can answer to this blueness?

D.H. Lawrence, of a gentian.[14]

Colours are visitations from the world of light. They melt into the surface of every thing and display the nobility of matter. Colours shake the eyes awake; they fish unlived thoughts and feelings to the surface of an ordinary day. The birds and trailing flowers of orange and yellow and midnight blue that lace their way around Tuscan cups and saucers, pots and plates, the humble ware of daily living, convey the light that hovers in the wings of any ordinary activity. Even the thought of blue and gold cloth in the midst of the grey of London can unveil a forgotten joy. Gold, the gold of an evening sun, the burnished yellow of a ripe cornfield, the gold leaf of an ageing basilica, even the rim of an old-fashioned dinner plate, can cast a fresh light on the day. Colours can reveal our luminous interior. Think of the pink flush inside a seashell, or the shimmer of mother-of-pearl, the purple blue of an iris, the silver of sun on water, the burning embers of a wood fire, the orange of an orange; turquoise and lapis lazuli, crimson silk in a sari shop, the bright flash of a Guatemalen hatband, marigolds, the sky just before dark, the royal blue of Byzantine mosaic, eyebright and bluebells, fresh green leaves unfurling in spring.

Look down any street in a Western city, however, and watch for the colour of the crowd. It will seem that variations of black and grey are the dominant style of the day. It has been said that where the Maoris can see hundreds of reds, and the Eskimos can see several shades of white, urban Westerners see hundreds of greys. Certainly black is a dominant colour in fashion. Black has power; it is a force to be reckoned with. It is a way of showing we are not to be taken lightly. Especially with padded shoulders and the universal appeal of leather. We're a mean bunch, and we live in a mean place, the rough and tumble of the modern city sprawl. Greys and blacks merge us into the background and allow us to flit like city-slicker shadows through the urban half-light.

Yet things are never as black as they seem: contrary to appearances, the imagination does not die. Its colours may seem to be eclipsed in a world of concrete, steel, and glass; but they manage still to sneak between the paving stones. People pour into print and poster shops to buy copies of Van Gogh's sunflowers, Gauguin's tropics, and Chagall's angels in their thousands. Among all the city shadows there are still radiant dresses fanning around female forms and flamboyant shirts in shop windows. People are as hungry as ever for colour. There are artists emerging today, as always, whose work proclaims the depth and brightness of another vision. Two artists in particular come to mind: Thetis Blacker,[15] and Andy Goldsworthy.[16]

Thetis Blacker's birds, beasts, and fishes do not come from the world of nature. They are vivid creatures of the imagination, not invented, but revealed to her in the world of dreams. 'Few can bring back the creatures of the mind into the waking world,' writes Kathleen Raine, 'but Thetis Blacker has the rare gift of summoning from their sanctuaries these oldest inhabitants of the human memory: not from the past, but from forgotten regions within ourselves.'[17] Blacker's medium is the dyed painting, batik, which she learned over many years in Java. Her series of bird paintings, called *The Search for the Simurgh*, are illustrations of scenes from the wonderful poem *The Conference of the Birds*, by the twelfth-century Persian poet, Attar.[18] Yet they are not illustrations in the literal sense: rather, as the artist herself says, they are 'punctuation marks, pauses for contemplation'. Her colours in this series, from orange to indigo, glow and burn like jewels. A print of one of them hangs in my home, and even this reproduction is like a lamp, permanently alight on the wall. A deep indigo bird, its graceful head turned towards a tail that swoops up in a curve to the air, is surrounded by a spiral of orange and yellow light that rivets the gaze. The eye is like a moth to such living colour as this.

Andy Goldsworthy's work captures the eye from another direction. He is, with Richard Long, one of Britain's foremost land artists. Whereas Long uses nature's shapes and forms, especially the circle, Goldsworthy takes the colours, as well as the forms of nature, and rearranges them so that we see what we have always seen in an entirely new way. His works are rarely to be found in galleries, but in the places where he makes them, from the North Pole to the Australian outback. Using the natural materials around him – twigs, leaves, stones, ice, wood – he builds forms of the utmost delicacy and beauty that follow the natural processes of nature, fading in time, or washing away with the elements. For the most part, then, Goldsworthy's work is to be seen in his own photographic record of it.

It is the shock of his colour that leaps out of the pages of those records. 'What counts most with colours,' said Matisse, 'are relationships. Colour attains its full expression only when it is organized; when it corresponds to the emotional intensity of the artist.'[19] In 1987 Goldsworthy laid rowan leaves, in their different stages of coloration, around a hole, in a circular quilt; the darker leaves at the periphery, edging into luminous red ones, which became orange by stages, and finally, around the circumference of the hole, a blaze of yellow. Looking upon the whole piece, it snatches the breath away. Then, in Japan, he stitched red maple leaves together to form a floating chain, snaking through rocks on the edge of some water. Such a simple thing, but who would have thought it: never have maple leaves been so red; never has red so opened my eye.

JOY, CREATIVITY, AND COMMITMENT

From joy springs all creation
By it is sustained,
Towards joy it proceeds
And to joy it returns
Mundaka Upanishad

&PILOGUE

When Eve left the womb of Paradise, she was never to return. Cherubim were placed at the Garden gates with flam-
ing swords to bar the way. But Eve never looked back; she
knew her destiny lay by another way. Her great work was to
find her own heaven on earth by the light of her own inner
eye. That is the riddle she puts to us now, for each of us to
answer in our own way.

We have certain clues. We know that good intentions are
not the answer, nor yet another project for the perfect
world. We know that countless political and religious ideal-
ists have littered our history with carnage. We know we are
alone, and that at the same time we only exist through relationship. We know that we live in the ceaseless ebb and
flow of union and separation, joy and sadness, and that we
cannot deny the one in favour of the other. Falling in love is
not enough on its own; neither is an independent course of
self-determination. The pathos of our predicament is Eve's
gift to us. Its bitter-sweetness is what runs in our veins and
flows through our senses in a ceaseless exchange with the
world.

In that exchange is another clue: that we let the current
flow; that we drink life down deeply and let it drink us in its
turn. There is a risk, of course: like the Japanese who love to

eat the poisonous puffer-fish, we don't know what the outcome will be. But there is also a joy. There are even moments
when the inner and the outer become one and the memory
of the riddle disappears. What a joy this is, sometimes quiet,
sometimes wild, the joy of being the world. Then, when we
feel we are all alone again, another clue is to remember that
our joy has not gone away: it is only on the other side of our
loneliness, which itself calls joy back into being. J.G. Bennett
says that

> There are periods one goes through when one is constantly
> aware of being bereft of something. When this feeling
> comes we have to watch over its purity and not misuse it.
> The feeling is itself authentic and is an indication of being
> near to something. One doesn't really feel deprived until
> one is close.[1]

Though the joy and the sadness will come and go, the more
we let the current of life through our senses the more we
may feel what it is like to belong. Belonging in the world,
sensing our kinship with it, gives rise to commitment; and
commitment is also a clue. Commitment is not something
we decide upon; something we try and direct towards
others, or demand from them. Commitment is an expression
of trust; and we trust when we sense we are of the same substance as another, and as the world. Knowing ourselves to
be of one body with life, suffused with it, we can throw ourselves wholeheartedly into the business of living it, without
any reason to hold back.

Given over to life, life can begin to play and have its creative way with us. The dominant Western model of creativity and art since the Renaissance has been that of the heroic individual struggling to make himself and his meaning out of his art. Yet when we already feel we belong to life, there is no meaning to look for or to try and create. The meaning is inherent in the process of life as it is happening, not apart from it, or behind it in some purer, transcendent realm. Then creativity happens for the sheer love of it, out of the abundance of life rather than from a desperate need to find meaning and value through 'expressing' oneself.[2] When, in this way, we join in the ongoing process of creating the world, we also assume some responsibility for it. This is the same responsibility that Eve took upon herself with the creative act of eating the apple. She wholly accepted the limitations and constraints of the world of matter, and set about illuminating it with the light of her knowing. Her knowing was the creative impulse which enabled her to see beyond the status quo. She could see through the names of things to the larger pattern of which they were a part. Eve's spontaneity transforms the simple activities of everyday life into art. It is in the creative aliveness we bring to being with our children; it is in the way we lay a table, make dinner, taste the food, make love with our partner, plant seeds, make pots, stitch clothes, look out of the window, listen to music, and smell the roses.

This creativity, joy, and commitment are all signs of a soul being forged in its embrace with the world – a soul which, in E.M. Forster's words,

> is the rainbow bridge that should connect the prose in us with the passion. Without it, we are meaningless fragments, half monks, half beasts, unconnected arches that have never joined into a man. The bridge would be built and span [our] lives with beauty.[3]

When, in each of us, the last stone of that bridge is in place, Eve's riddle will finally be solved.

$\mathcal{N}$OTES

The Erotic Life

1. Quoted by Keith Sagar in *The Life of D.H. Lawrence* (Methuen, 1980).
2. See Robert Johnson, *She: Understanding Feminine Psychology* (Harper, San Francisco, 1976) for an excellent rendering of the Eros story.
3. For a fuller version of how the Church proceeded to outlaw Eros, see Matthew Fox, *Original Blessing* (Bear & Co., 1983).
4. J.G. Bennett, *The Way To Be Free* (Coombe Springs Press, 1971)

Tasting

1. Published by Macmillan, 1990; p.353.
2. Marion Woodman is one of North America's leading Jungian psychologists. See her books *Addiction to Perfection* (Inner City Books, 1983); *The Ravaged Bridegroom* (Inner City Books, 1990); and *The Pregnant Virgin* (Inner City Books, 1985).
3. P.D. Ouspensky, *In Search of the Miraculous* (Routledge & Kegan Paul, 1950), p.181.
4. Sul-Minerva, the Roman goddess of healing.
5. See Thich Nhat Hanh's books, published by Shambala: *Miracle of Mindfulness; Breath, You Are Alive;* and *The Sun My Heart.*
6. René Daumal, *Mt Analogue* (Penguin).
7. Gabrielle Roth, dancer, musician, and author of *Maps to Ecstasy* (Harper Collins, 1989).

Smelling

1. Translated by John E. Woods (Penguin, 1987), pp.35-6.
2. I had heard of this tick already, but reading of it in Susskind's novel *Perfume* brought home to me what a powerful symbol of smell the creature is. My description of it is a rendering of Susskind's.
3. See the section on smell in Diane Ackerman's *A Natural History of the Senses* (Random House, 1990).
4. Max Lake, *Scents and Sensuality* (Futura, 1991).
5. Ibid.
6. Ibid., p.12.
7. Ibid.
8. Daniele Ryman, *Aromatherapy* (Piatkus, 1991), p.5
9. Ibid.
10. In the *Independent*, 5 May 1992.
11. From the 'My Turn' column, *Newsweek*, 21 March 1988. Quoted in *A Natural History of the Senses*, p.41
12. Quoted ibid., p.17.
13. Quoted in *Scents and Sensuality*, pp.7-8.
14. Quoted ibid., p.16.
15. *A Natural History of the Senses*, p.22.
16. For all these, see *Scents and Sensuality*, p.16.
17. Ram Dass, *How Can I Help?* (Rider, 1991), p.120.
18. *Paradiso*, Canto 23 lines 73-5. For this and other 'saintly' smells mentioned, see 'Of the Good Odours, and the Odour of the Good' in F. Gonzalez-Crussi's *The Five Senses* (Picador, 1990).
19. H.W.L. Poonja is in his eighties and lives in Lucknow.
20. Andrew Harvey, *Love's Fire: Re-Creations of Rumi* (Jonathan Cape, 1988). Jalaludin Rumi, one of the greatest saints and poets of Islam,

lived in the thirteenth century.
21. *Independent Magazine*, 11 April
1992.
22. There is, however, a formidable
and influential group that is trying to
bring the soul of Dallas awake. The
Dallas Institute offers a wide range of
cultural courses as well as helping the
city fathers to see with fresh
perspectives. See their booklet,
Imagining Dallas (The Pegasus
Foundation, 1982).
23. *A Natural History of the Senses*,
p.36.
24. *Love's Fire.*

Touching
1. *The Letters of D.H. Lawrence*,
Volume 1 (Cambridge University
Press), p.30.
2. Published by Penguin Arkana.
3. *A Natural History of the Senses*, p.73.
4. Ibid., p.123.
5. See his book, *Birth Without Violence*
(Mandarin, 1991).
6. See his books, *Birth Reborn*
(Souvenir, 1984); *Entering the World*
(Marian Boyars, 1989); and *Water and
Sexuality* (Penguin Arkana, 1990).
7. Dr Christopher Nyrop, *The Kiss in
History*, quoted in *A Natural History of
the Senses*, p.110.
8. See Salman Rushdie's description
of his childhood in 'Imaginary
Homelands', *Granta* (Penguin, 1991).
9. A Christian contemplative who
affirms the universal wisdom
common to all spiritual traditions,
and who has spent extended periods
in Zen monasteries. See his book,
Gratefulness: The Heart of Prayer
(Paulist Press, New York, 1984).
10. Quoted in *D.H. Lawrence: A
Selection* ed. R.H. Poole and P.J.
Shepherd (Heinemann, 1990). p.3.
11. Peter Brook, *The Shifting Point*
(Methuen, 1988), p.232.
12. Peter Brook, *A Theatrical Casebook*
(Methuen, 1988), p.375.
13. Norman O. Brown, quoted in *The
Pregnant Virgin*, p.54.
14. Ibid., p.179.

Listening

1. Quoted in *A Natural History of
Senses*, p.191.
2. Don Gifford, *The Farther Shore: A
Natural History of Perception* (Faber &
Faber, 1990), p.59.
3. For a full and beautifully told
account of the diminishment of the
listening ear and the rising
domination of the eye, see *The Farther
Shore*. See also Joachim Ernst Berendt,
The Third Ear (Element, 1990).
4. Published by Picador, 1990.
5. The Open Gate is a programme of
conferences on the arts, psychology
and cultural developments. For
details, write to The Open Gate, 6
Goldney Road, Bristol BS8 4RB.
6. Chandra Swami lives near Dehra
Dun in India.
7. Published by Vintage, 1985.
8. *Wordsworth: Poetical Works* (Oxford
University Press, 1990), p.382.
9. Published by Floris Books.
10. Michael Ende, *Momo* (Penguin,
1984), p.17.
11. Ibid., p.21.
12. This Ram Dass story may be in
How Can I Help?, although I cannot
trace it. I tell it from memory.
13. See D.W. Winnicott's books,
Home Is Where We Start From
(Penguin, 1990); and *The Child, the
Family, and the Outside World*
(Penguin, 1991).
14. Robert Bly is a poet, storyteller,
and inspiration for the men's
movement. His books include *Iron
John* (Element, 1992), and *A Little Book
on the Human Shadow* (Element, 1992).
15. Maurice O'Sullivan, *Twenty Years
A-Growing* (Oxford University Press,
1976).
16. Aster Aweke is known to all
Ethiopians. She has lived in the
United States for the last ten years.
Her music appears in the United
Kingdom on the Triple Earth label.
17. Trio Bulgaka, *Les Mystères des Voix
Bulgares*, on the 4 AD label.
18. Richard Lannoy, *The Speaking Tree*
(Oxford University Press, 1971).
19. 'Imaginary Homelands'.
20. *The Third Ear.*
21. The Tomatis Centre, 68 Blvd des

Coumelles, Paris 75017.
22. R.J. Stewart, *Music and the Elemental Psyche* (Aquarian), p.119.
23. Among his many recordings are *Eternity; La Flute de Hari Prasad;* and *Hari Prasad in Concert*.

Seeing
1. Quoted by Jack D. Flann in *Matisse on Art* (Phaidon), p.51.
2. Richard Kearney, *The Wake of Imagination* (Hutchinson Educational, 1988), p.3
3. *The Farther Shore.*
4. *The Wake of Imagination*, p.1.
5. *The Farther Shore*, p.30.
6. J.G. Bennett, *The Image of God in the Work* (Coombe Springs Press, 1976), p.48.
7. For a superb inquiry into the various dimensions of romantic love, see John Haule, *Divine Madness* (Shambala, 1990).
8. Ananda Mayi Ma, an Indian saint who died in 1982.
9. *Joseph Campbell and the Power of Myth*, Tape 5 'Love and the Goddess' (Mystic Fire Audio, PO Box 9323, South Burlington, Vermont VT05403, USA.
10. D.W. Winnicott.
11. Irene Tweedie is the author of *Chasm of Fire* (Element).
12. Quoted by Susan Sontag in *On Photography* (Penguin, 1977). Much of this section is inspired by Sontag's book, which is as relevant today as when it was written.

13. Quoted ibid.
14. Quoted in *The Life of D.H. Lawrence.*
15. Thetis Blacker studied the fabric arts of Southeast Asia in Indonesia. Her sixteen banners on *Genesis* and the *Apocalypse* were commissioned for the 900th anniversary of Winchester Cathedral. She is the author of *A Pilgrimage of Dreams*.
16. Andy Goldsworthy is one of Europe's foremost land artists. The circle of rowan leaves round a hole can be seen in *Andy Goldsworthy* (Viking, 1990).
17. *Temenos*, No.4 p.117, available from Temenos, 47 Paulton Square, London SW3 5DT.
18. Translated by Afkham Darbands and Dick Davis (Penguin Classics, 1984). Peter Brook made a stage production of the poem in 1979 for the Avignon Festival. Attar was a Sufi, and his poem allegorizes the human condition and mankind's search for truth.
19. *Matisse on Art*.

Joy, Creativity, and Commitment
1. *The Way To Be Free.*
2. For a fuller description of this kind of creativity, see the chapter 'The Two Faces of Creativity' in Morris Berman's *Coming To Our Senses* (Bantam, 1990).
3. *Howard's End* (Penguin).